Capturing Life and Movement en Plein Air

By Deborah Chapin
Master Plein Air Painter

Capturing Life and movement en Plein air

Definitive art book on painting on location.

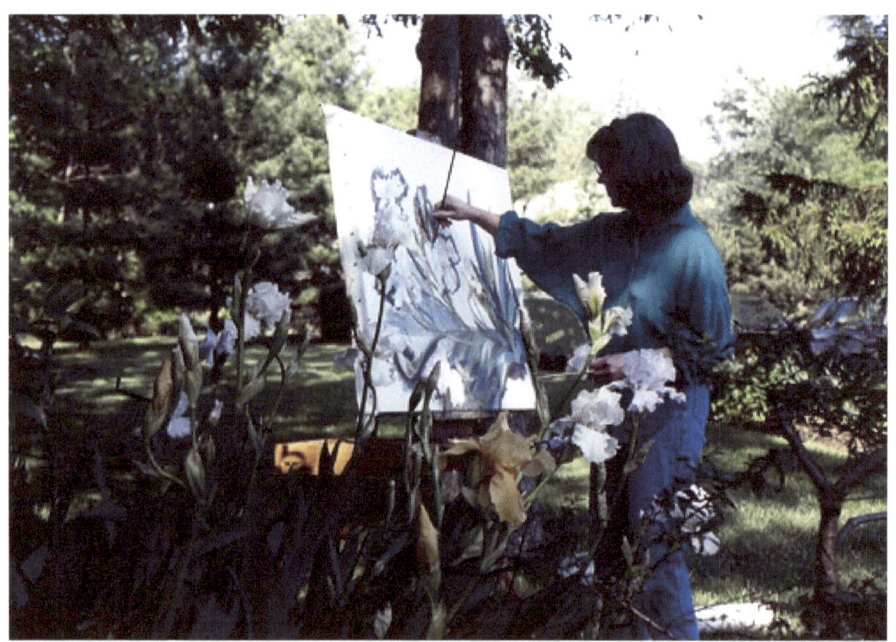

Acknowledgments

I would like to thank my friends for sharing their ideas during our art discussions during this writing.   Particularly I would like to thank Pierre Rioux for his encouragement to publish.   He was instrumental in making this book a reality and his help is greatly appreciated. I would also like to thank my mother for her caring support despite being techno-challenged during this project. I hope the reader finds this guide useful and informative and I encourage readers to engage in dialogue about the honorable profession of plein air painting. By doing so, you will discover a wonderful world within.

Third edition
ISBN 13: 978-0-9825354-3-1 NHStudios Press

https://Gallery.DeborahChapin.com
Published by Chapin studio at Stoneridge
24 Stoneridge Ln., Bristol, ME 04539

Contents:

Nature's basics:

Introduction

When I started painting full-time portraying competitive sailing (10 Years), I found the subject of small boats exciting to paint; all that action on the water, between the water swirling around the boats and the sailors racing their hearts out. I used to used photos because the subject matter was on the water. This was a good way to get started on a complex subject such as this, but it has less to do with what I eventually discovered Fine Art to be. I learned a great deal about movement, water as a subject, and a perspective during this time. But my teacher insisted that wasn't all there was to painting. She kept telling me that if I just go out and paint on site, my work would improve a thousand fold. She was right! Although I went through an initial shock of disappointing results, as I've learned to paint directly from nature, I noticed something almost immediately. There was nothing like it! One is put in a veritable pea soup of activity; life was teaming all around with sounds, smells, action, action and more action. Here everything moved; the light, the color, lines, subjects, even the air moved. I was connected to a life force, that although I had spent a great deal of time outside, I'd never before noticed. This is what plein air painting is all about. Life in movement, the connection to it and the translation of it into paint.

This book teaches you how to capture that life and how to see that movement, and how to remember it accurately in your mind. I'll give you a plan of attack for any on-site work. You will learn about brushwork; how to discern what to keep, what to modify; about light and color; how do use it to create a design within design; and how to compose movement in apparently still subjects. In the end, you will know what plein air painting really means and understand what has captivated artists since it's beginning in France

"The studio artist has complete control over his/her model and lighting/ environment. The plein air artist must take the elements as they are and re-create the subject, given the factors presented. Of course, the immediately obvious conclusion is that this control factor, or lack thereof, would be one of the main reasons for the divergence between studio and plein air painting and the character of collectors who are drawn to them."

Deborah Chapin

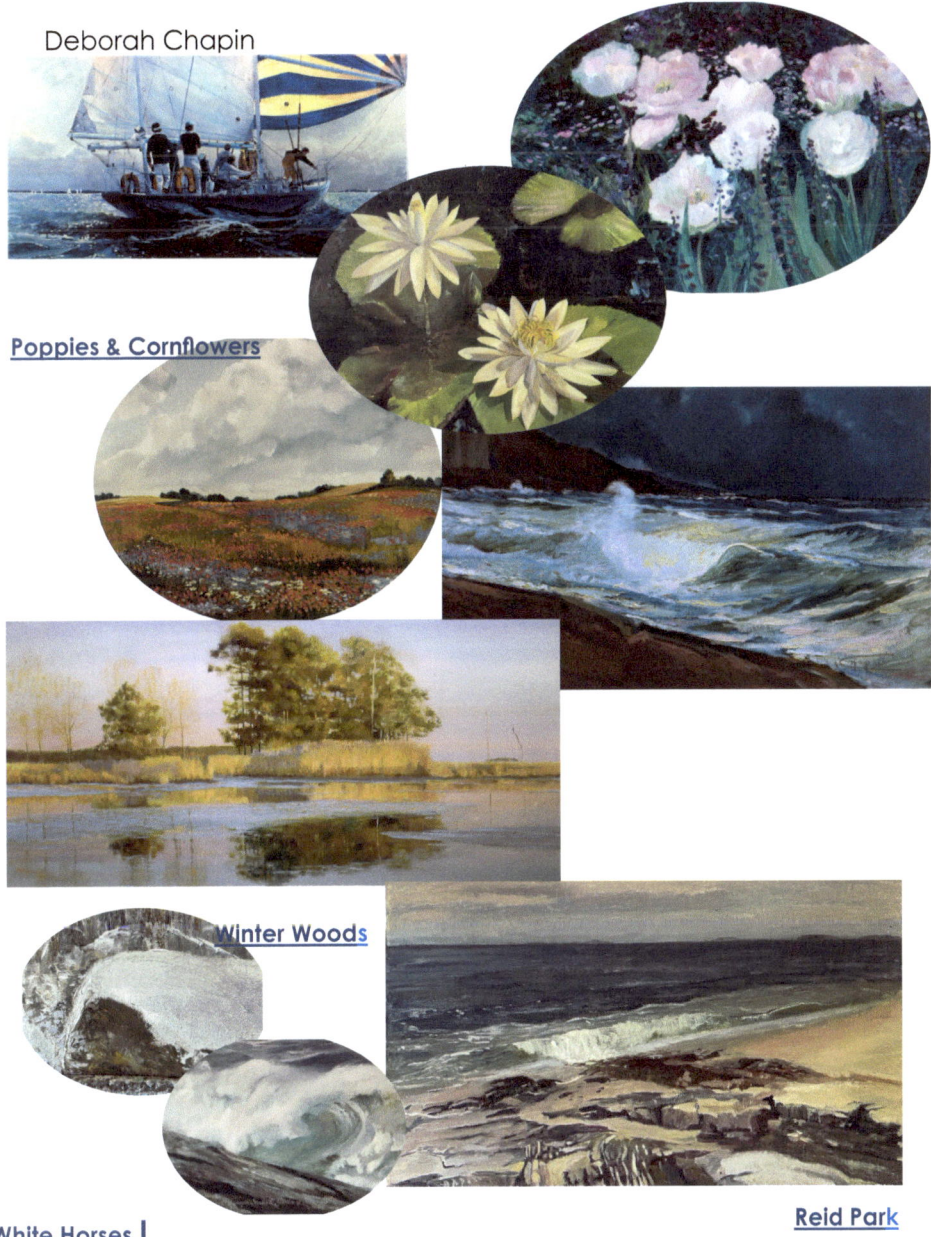

Poppies & Cornflowers

Winter Woods

White Horses I

Reid Park

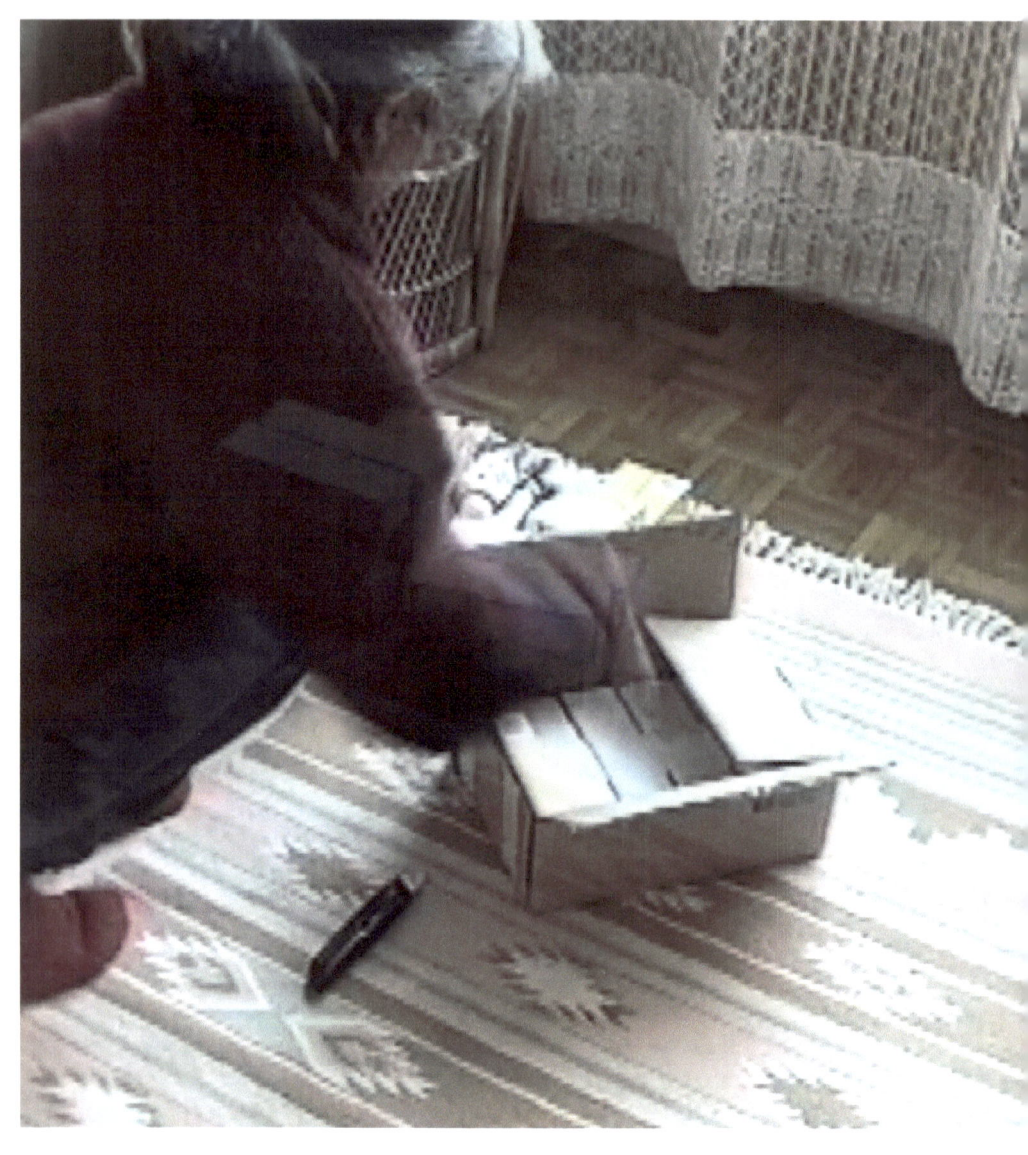

See the full process in a time-lapse movie

Preparation for the trip

One of my main nemesis of making trips to France, or any location, is luggage. Every year upon arrival I have the impression that the airport has been evacuated. Not a soul to be seen anywhere near my baggage, which includes on any stay or of duration; three duffel bags of artist materials; one suitcase with easel inside; one carton Roughly the size of a trombone case and two pieces of carry-on luggage. Still, all seven bags are easier to manipulate, weighing in at 40 - 75 pounds each, then the two large crates I built and hauled around the first year.

Duffel in fact, includes 35 canvases - already cut to size is that will be usable with my stretcher bars; four boxes (not tubes) of each oil color; an assortment of brushes numbering around 200; some reading materials; an easel, some basic supplies and wherever packaging is required, a modicum of clothing. I might have another duffel bag to carry stretcher bars.

Before when can begin to paint, however, canvases must be stretched. There are two main reasons for an artist to bring her own supplies Pre-9/11.

1. Economy: I saw an approximately 20 x 30" stretched canvas of roughly the same quality as mine in a Paris shop costing Fr.400 which at the time of this writing is roughly $66 note that in 2022 it would be about $142. That's one canvas I have 35.

2. It is not always possible to purchase a particular product at any given location.

I prefer stretched canvas to board because of the touch. I think the artist loses her sensitivity to the surface, painting on a board and hence the brushwork suffers. It is also lighter than board and when you are traveling this is a plus.

Before painting, the canvas must be prepared for the field, i.e. the canvas must be toned. Toning is the graying down of the canvas with the sienna ground upon which to paint.

The artist does this because when surrounded by bright sunlight and reflective surfaces such as the sea and sand it helps the eyes not to have an additional bright surface such as a white canvas. Also, if the artist tones a canvas the same color as the palette, it facilitates the seeing of color on the palette and the canvas since the foundation color is the same. In addition, this foundation may be used as part of the subject creating a negative space, which adds part of the subject and plays with the viewer's eyes and mind. It looks like a painted surface when in fact it is not.

The easel must also be reassembled and packed with paints, though not necessarily in that order. You may forget this, by loading it up with brushes and paint before attaching the legs, as I frequently do. The easel of choice is the Julien French easel because, despite some frustrations with the hardware, it is still the most durable and utilitarian for all conditions in the field. The three legs can be wedged between rocks without fear of scuffing up a delicate surface or losing some high-tech gizmo. This easel has withstood 48 kn of wind with a full size canvas on it. Lighter is not always better. It holds canvases from 3" x 5" minis - 30" x 40" Maxis. Its weakest feature, the hardware, can be replaced. Because of the abuse that I put my equipment through, no other modern contraption could hold up to the conditions that I paint in.

Each time a painting is completed and dry to the touch it is taken off the stretcher bars and a new canvas is then stretched in its place and the whole process is repeated. All pennies are re-stretched immediately upon return to my workshop at home. The system allows me to paint 30+ pieces with only 7 to 10 sets of stretcher bars.

Suggested supply list and packing suggestions.

- Easel: I use the Julien easel, pack it in a square suitcase with foam around it and put it on the plane just like luggage. Whatever you do, pack it so it doesn't rock around with rough treatment.

- Satchel bag: for carrying a roll of paper towels, bottle of drinking water, snacks etc.... do not get anything too nice, it will have turpentine paint and dirt on it by the end of the week. You can use a large Ziploc bag and then backpack anywhere with both hands free.

- Palette: I recommend in the wooden palette that comes with most French easels. Be sure that it is cured with oil in advance of the trip. Do not use any white palettes. Or paper palettes. Or plastic palettes. It will blind you and make it difficult to judge your colors.

- Paints: I use Old Holland oil colors because of their pigmentation and it is pure color ground in cold pressed linseed oil. There is a great discrepancy between one brand on another and so realize that when I instruct you on mixing colors your results may be different with a different brand.My palette.

  - Three blues Include: French blue or Cobalt Blue, Prussian blue, cerulean blue.

  - Three yellows include: cadmium yellow or Talens yellow, ochre, And maybe your lemon yellow.

  - Two-Four reds alizarin crimson, burnt sienna, magenta (specific flowers) and Rose madder (only for flowers)

- Turpentine: paper towels and bottled water. Buy yourself one of the steel cans, sealed that have a metal bin for washing out brushes in turpentine called an airtight brush washer which you can purchase at ASW or any of the art stores. Turpentine is made out of the resin from trees. There is nothing particularly unsustainable about it except that it is pretty smelly. You can all also use the non smelly version.

- Brushes: I recommend at least three in each size of the following except the larger brushes. The reason for this is to work in a light middle and dark tone all at once and still keep your colors clean. The exceptions are larger brushes. One of these would be sufficient unless you want to make a significant investment. Do not use old worn out brushes, it will not help you.

  - Rafael white bristle filberts number #3572 in sizes 6, 8, 12, and 18.

  - Rafael rounds #8772 in size is 6, 4 and 2

  - And then for finer work I'm currently using Winsor Newton silver it's called Rathbone in sizes #2, 4, 6

- Canvas: for a long trip use heavy duty Ponderosa Stretcher bars so that I can take a couple of sets and a lot of canvas, stretch in new ones for the day and rotate the stretched canvases. I can also recommend the canvas pads for practice, which are canvas in a pad cut to size for practice sessions. You can leave your stretcher pliers at home and can just have a couple of bulldog clips to clip it to a board and when you are finished whoosh onto the next canvas. However, I strongly recommend stretching the canvases when you are back at home or mounting onto boards for those works you wish to keep... Also pick a heavier canvas for most outdoor work due to the winds in elements that you contend with most of the time; these are subject to humidity too.

- Suggestions on how to pack supplies. I suggest you have one suitcase or duffel bag for clothes and one for supplies in a separate suitcase for your easel. Check with your airlines for size and weight restrictions for luggage. Make sure your suitcase for your supplies is able to carry canvases and paint snugly. I packed my brushes in the French easel and this seems to be OK but I put my paints in a box and packed it in a duffel bag. Be sure you can lift the bag! Because there are no porters anymore.

- Clothes to pack: generally weather conditions will dictate to each person according to a personal preference in the climate in which he or she is painting.

However be sure to include the following: One sun hat. Three pairs of painting pants and jeans are good for protection in rough environments. A couple of sweaters for cooler conditions next to the sea, a heavier one and one light weight. Something to wear touring. A rain poncho or windbreaker. One sturdy pair of well broken in comfortable walking working shoes, thick socks which go halfway up the calf to cover the ankles and bottom of the pant legs, protection against spiders and ticks. Some sort of bug repellent which works for you. I use a spray "deep woods off" to douse the hat in this as well. Variety of cotton shirts for warm weather if applicable breath mints, toothbrush, deodorant don't forget the amenities.

- Healthcare particulars: if you are used to exercise and standing for 2 to 3 hours, good! You'll need to get into shape if you are not. Also, I recommend carrying a small tube of Benadril gel in case you have reactions to bug bites like I do. Depending on where you are traveling. Carrying any medical supplies with you.

- I used a pelican case number 1620 to carry smaller wet canvases. If you are serious this is a good way to go. It is sturdy, has wheels and extended handles like hard side luggage only it's made for transporting things safely; my photographer friends put me onto them. They are an investment but they'll last forever and they are a lot cheaper than a metal case used for shipping sealed luggage. You can make a wet canvas carrier out of a double corrugated cardboard and then recycle it when you are through. If you are only doing a short two week trip, just pile up a batch of canvases into your box one on top of the other with spacers between the canvases. The stretcher bars actually separate the paintings faces from one another. To stabilize the batch of canvas you can duct tape the sides of the pile together making a block of canvases see illustration. You can box already made Masonite boards but they aren't cheap and consider the weight of Masonite boards; I don't recommend this. If you do this you are limited to working in the sizes the box manufacturer makes. Another method I've seen work is mounting different size canvas pieces on foam core leaving Borders for stretching canvas later varying the size you'd like to work on but keeping the foam boards the same size. For this you need to separate your finished work by gluing on taped pieces of boards eraser to the front edges of your canvas remember to mask out the edges of your canvas before you begin painting. Then pull off before the painting dries also double stick tape to tack the canvas onto your support and voilà!

… A modern influence, to which painters are subjected, is the lack of appreciation for the quiet mood piece. It seems to struggle to gain a voice at this time. As an artist I ask myself why? The role of imagination in the creation and observation of art has become diminutive. Our bustling society is always on the go in a frenzied pace, which only seems to increase, rather than diminish, with modern conveniences. We don't take time to cultivate our minds nor expand our knowledge base. Modern marketing techniques have also run amok, pelting us with the bazaar in the glitzy in an attempt to capture our attention, rather than utilizing qualities of uniqueness and beauty. As artists we must be careful to guard our sensibilities to those things which are subtle, unique and beautiful, letting nature be our primary guide. Otherwise our contributions as artists are reduced to little more than repetition of commercial formulas.

"It's a question of influence," By Deborah Chapin

Preparation for the field

Nuts and Bolts checklist of considerations before heading out:

- Prepare your canvas by toning it. This will keep glare down out in the field. A mixture of burnt sienna and French blue works well in a medium tone. Prepare the night before painting so that it is dry.

- Preparing the easel: make sure that you have a tube of each color for use in the field and put blobs of paint on the palette so that you are ready to go.

- Handy tools for emergencies: I have found it helpful to have a case of bolts locking up on my easel to carry a small hammer and needle nose pliers. Sometimes wood swells in the beach and sea environments and the hammer can be used to collapse the legs of your easel. Needle nose pliers are good to loosen frozen bolts and screws on the easel. This happens frequently with an easel that is under stress from wind and weather and humidity.

- Preparing the artist: consider the hike and or climb to reach the location you're going to paint. If it includes a hike, try to make the easel set up as light as possible. An easel weighs 40 pounds with brushes and paint. If the hike includes a number of narrow ledges, you'll want to consider the size of your canvas. This is also an important consideration when the wind is a factor. A 20 x 30 canvas acts as a sail attached to your easel and can exert considerable force if caught in the wind, enough to knock you down.

- Types of canvas to use. I use heavy Belgian linen canvas in the field, in particular Galacia. I started out with a lighter weight canvas but soon discovered that the heavier weave stretched less and stayed taunt in windy conditions.

- You must've assure yourself that your easel is functional, it won't fall apart or collapse on you by losing bolts and latches. Fix it if you have any doubts by using Epoxy glue.

- Are you warmly enough dressed to stand stationary several hours next to the sea or in the early morning dew of a field? Are you dressed in layers so that you can shed layers as the day goes on? If you are painting where there are bugs have you applied bug repellent? With Deep woods Off nothing wants to get next to you after you spray that on yourself. I find that if I spray my hat and put it on it does two things it keeps the sun out of my eyes and the mosquitoes and Gnats out of my face. After 2 to 3 hours of a Seascape or Landscape, with all the accompanying frustrations, will you be able to complete the prerequisite hike back up the cliff or down the path? This is not as easy as it sounds. Concentration on the level needed uses up a lot of energy, which is required to accomplish these works, combined with normal physical demand, which occurs when anyone is hiking and standing, consumes enormous amounts of energy. Oil painting en plein air, if one follows in the footsteps of the impressionist, is not for ninnies.

Preparation for Painting

- The main consideration in preparation for painting is the painting idea... The better you know a place, the more creative your concepts will become. I develop these ideas from one year to the next. For example, if I find a location that has yielded winners in the past, I make a point of trying different combinations. If you paint a winner in the morning light on a breezy day the same subject forms may be also beautiful in the late afternoon with the lazy wafting breeze or the still calm of dawn. One of the reasons for bringing loads of materials i.e. canvases and paint with you is that you won't feel inhibited about doing a painting that you're not sure is going to work, and risk failure. Seasons of the year evolve, the vegetation's coloration changes, shapes change according to rotation of crops through the different fields, or as a result of snow, ice or wind. So the first year I might try out an idea by making color sketches; the second year exploring in greater depth seeing that different fields have been planted and that after a particularly harsh winter what the vegetation looks like. The third year, if ideas have yielded good work, I might expand to larger works and continue to develop my understanding and enhance my interpretation in paint. So each idea develops out of an original inspiration, and increases with understanding as the idea matures and develops in an evolutionary process.

- When considering a setting for a painting ask yourself these questions:

    1. What would it look like back lit?

    2. What happens to it when the wind moves through it?

    3. What happens when cloud shadows pass over it

The Mindset:

- The other major element of preparation necessary for painting is a mindset. I generally prepare by focusing or reflecting on a piece that I've already accomplished of a similar subject or day, reminding myself of what I've accomplished before.   When sees this when painting movement, as there is a certain barrier to overcome and "capturing" this element.   I also search for the most spectacular scenes, which have a significant impact on the site on me. I like that "hit me in the face" experience. You are building momentum for tackling the painting just like a runner prepares for a race.   When the runner gets ready and set, there's nothing worse than a false start. This is what happens when a tourist arrives just after you were setting up. Tourists may break the concentration and literally halt the momentum or flow. No offense to Tourists.

Prior research increasing the odds:

- Sometimes you do just happen on a perfect site. However, my approach is to learn more about the environment and increase the odds by finding something really worth painting. Research for painting begins in the mind of the artist. I have a lot of ideas that I'd like to see realized in paint. The more experience an artist has, the more plausible the ideas become and the more successful one becomes to find an idea realized in the landscape, seascape or garden. You'll find that you want to paint instead of just settling serendipity.

Checklist for increasing the odds

- Lay of the land, in conjunction with different lighting conditions.

- If I'm doing a Seascape, I consider the tide with its rise and fall in relationship to the time of day angle of light.

- If I'm painting a harbor or inlet, I study its orientation to the sun.

- If I want to accomplish larger work, the location must be relatively easy to reach.

- The subject must be situated at the right angle to the light, if I want to use back lighting or reflected light.

- If I'm painting subjects such as poppies, I study what conditions have been present in order to pick a good year.

- If you were looking for cloud shadows, look for a day when there are puffy cumulus clouds moving through the sky. Weather forecast can give you ideas of when this will happen.

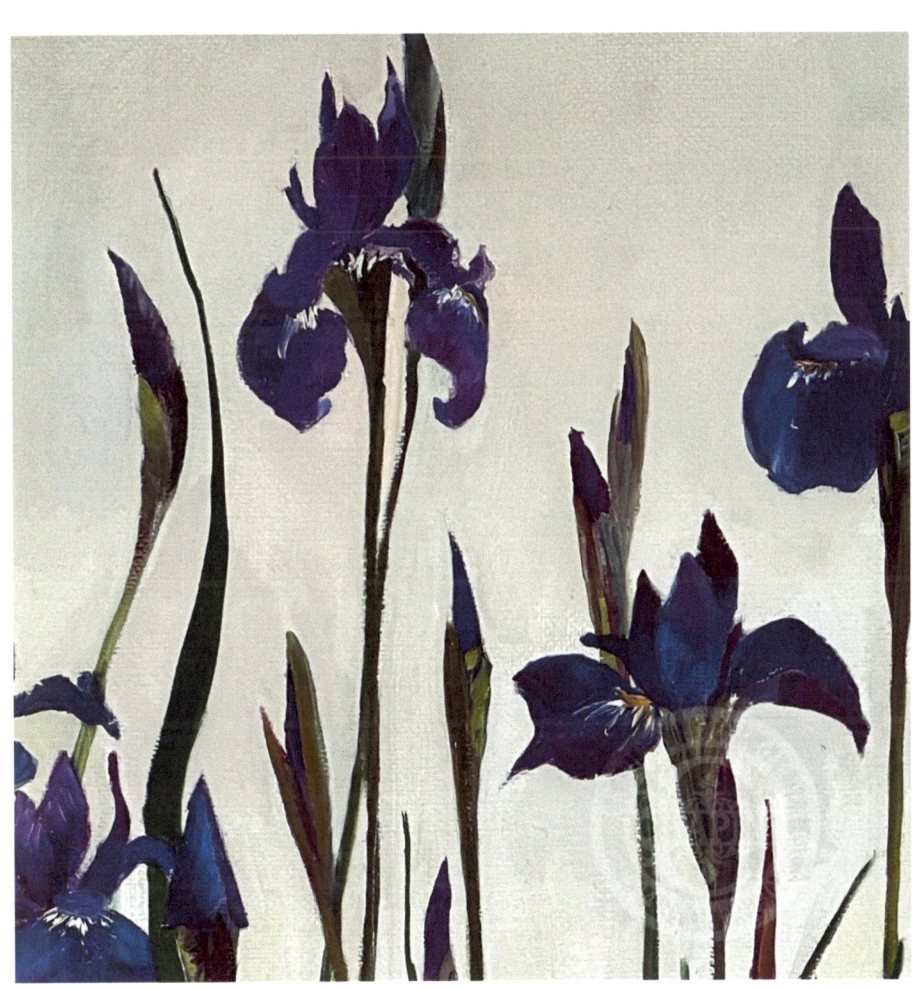

Blue Siberian

A portrait of the woods is more than the mirror snapshot. A snapshot is a static dead thing of 1/1000 of a second. But when you paint the woods, you can interpret that moment through your feelings and emotions about the woods, and use all the years of your accumulated experience. This is the greatest advantage the painters have over photographers and it is what we lose when we start using snapshots from which to paint. Painting on site allows artist chance to regain their edge and their niche. When you paint the woods, you're painting must look like all woods that have ever grown and have something deeper to say than a Kodak moment. When I see a brook in the woods I remember happy hours of fishing with my father; having to call him to untangle my line; watching my black lab frolicking in the stream and scaring the fish away; dazzling sunlight dancing on the surface; freezing my toes when wading in to bring in my prize; cooking the trout over an open fire; smells of smoke; cold winds and warm sunny days. There is so much more to say about nature than what just meets the eye, the heart must be allowed to speak as well.

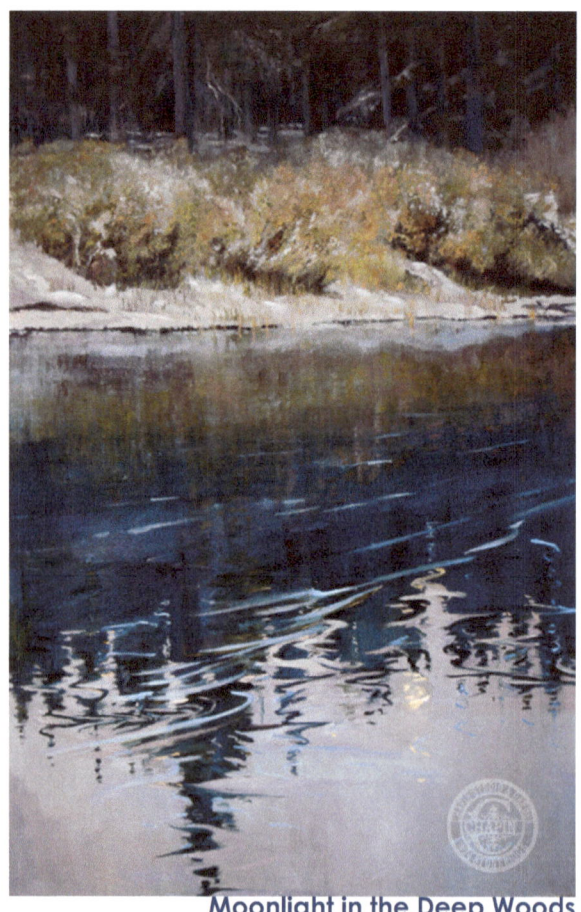

Moonlight in the Deep Woods

Debbie's rules of painting

- **First rule:** paint what inspires you. How do you know this? When you see something, which interest you, analyze what it is about the subject (light, lines, color) that triggers are response in you! That is what you want to search for in your subjects. When you find the keys you'll be able to consciously seek out these elements to unlock your subjects. You'll find that your interest level skyrockets. There's nothing like the impulse of paint to make a painting perk.

- **Second rule:** if you're not satisfied with the results, scrape it off right then and there. Do not wait for someone else to frown at it.

- **Third rule:** Study your subject of choice. Make it your passion. Understand it's very roots, and get to know it intimately. Spend time observing it without a brush. Then paint it over and over and over again. I have probably painted several 1000 successful and unsuccessful Marines and water related pieces over my career to date make that 10 times that. I can still say there are many things about the subject which I find challenging and which I do not quite understand. Still I can trace Water movements in my mind. Get to know that the very character of the irises are or the trees or the grass or the sunlight on sand or the sea whatever you choose to paint. Do it so well that your piece says something to you every time you look at it. Fall in love with it. If it can do this for you it will do that for others.

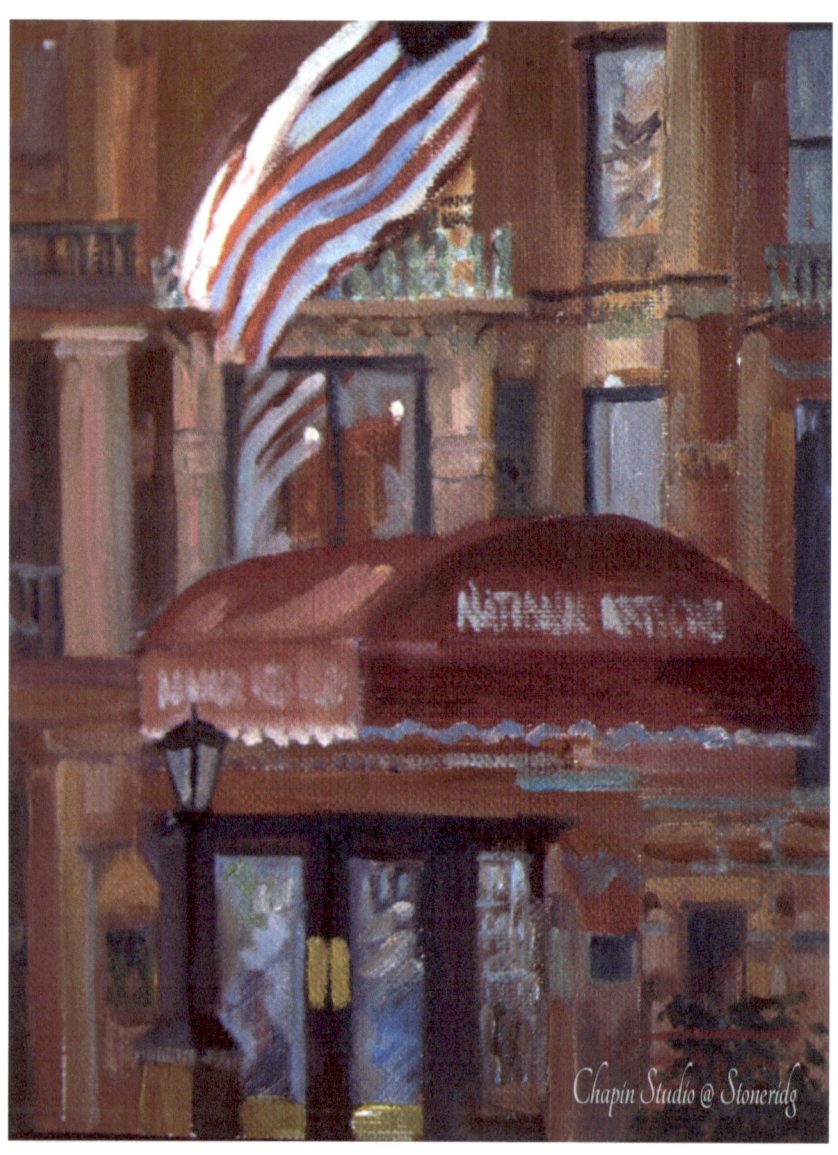

Chapin Studio @ Stoneridg

Nature's color

How nature uses color:

I have my own theory of color which I have been teaching for a number of years and whenever I give this demonstration, people become fascinated with the use of color. It is especially revealing to see color apart from color wheels and theory. One can truly understand what makes it work, what makes it harmonize and what gives it subtleties. People, who paint in pure color all over the canvas, are leaving the viewer with a little chance to rest. This is a direct result of our over commercialized existence. These people do not understand color, for they show their wares too readily and leave no mystery to be discovered.

In nature, there are no color wheels. It is better to understand what nature is doing. Comprehending this you will be able to succeed wherever you set up your easel. There are several secrets, which I have discovered over the years, some of which are following;

- **First,** the main trick of nature is your combinations of opposites when coming to color or light or line.

- **Secondly,** all of the colors change in harmony with the color of the light. So if the light is cool all the colors of the landscape/ seascape shift to the cooler colors or bluer cast. The opposite is true if you're painting mid day when the temperatures of the light are at its warmest or whitest.

- **Thirdly,** nature uses contrast in a myriad of ways, not only color opposites, but warm versus cool, subtle versus brilliant and light versus dark. She also does it in a combination with major elements versus details, and strong effects contrasted with soft effects.

Warm versus cool colors definition: When talking about warm color versus cool color what do I mean? Any color combinations such as green can have a warm or a cool cast. If the yellow dominates that it's a warm cast if the blue dominates it's a cool cast. Additionally, you can have different color temperatures based on the mixing, i.e. how pure the color is. For example, a green mixture with a warmer yellow, such as cadmium yellow would be warmer than a green mixture with a grayer yellow such as Naples or Ochre.

Gray and its definition: Grays defined by the following; anytime, you mix all three primary colors together i.e. yellow, blue, and red. Colors can be mixed in any proportion so technically a secondary color i.e. Violet,

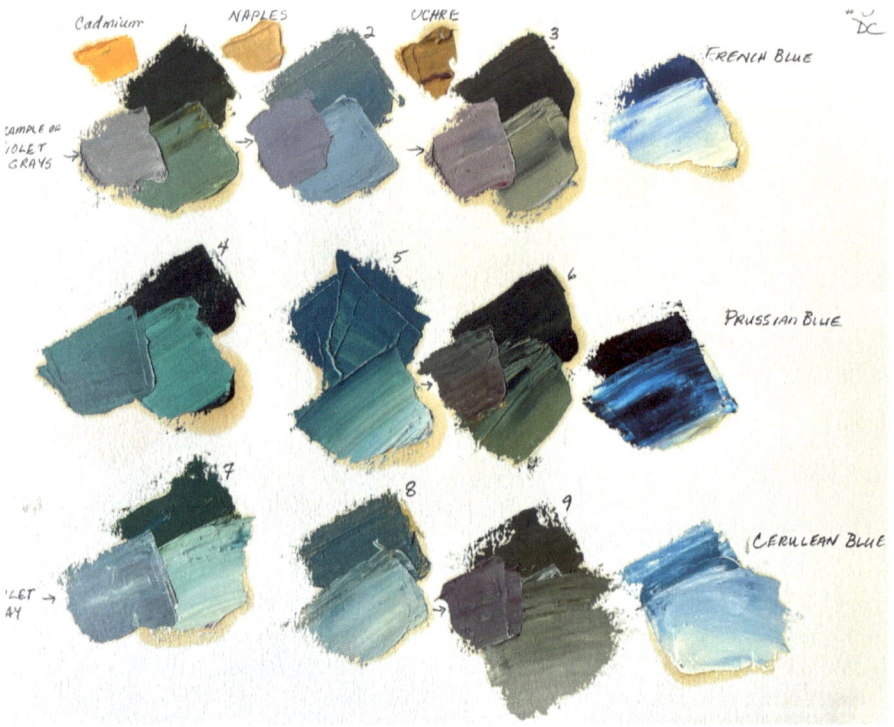

orange or green can be grayed by adding a third primary missing from the triangle even in very minute quantities and still be considered a gray.

For example: if you have a violet you can gray it by adding just a touch of yellow. Nature mixes her grays in brilliant forms and in a subtler forms and she combines them which creates contrasts in the Landscape or Seascape.

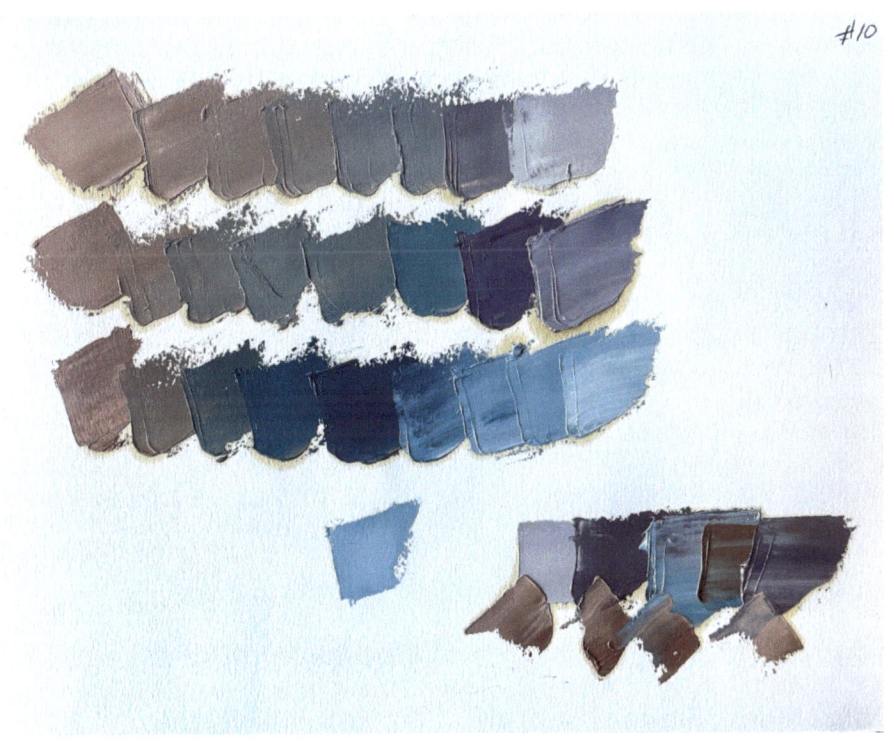

So, blue and red make violet. Add a touch of yellow to gray down.

Red and yellow make orange. And it had a touch of blue to grade down.

Blue and yellow make green. Add a touch of red to gray it down.

My palette:

The first point I want to make, at this juncture, is that I use Old Holland brand oil paints. I chose to switch to these paints because they are composed of all natural pigments. Also the pigments are very dense. They are ground in cold pressed linseed oil, which has historically been proven to be the best method for conservation of color and paintings over time. BTW linseed oil comes out of the flax plant which is also used to make linen. It is grown for this purpose. It is not the oil out of the ground.

Therefore, if you do the exercises below I recommend getting a tube of each of the following to actually see the colors which I am discussing. If you want to try and reinvent the colors with your particular favorite brand, realize that not all burnt sienna's are alike etc....

My palette, as laid out below, consists of three blues, three yellows and two red and white

Blues: Cerulean Blue, French blue, Prussian blue

Yellows: Naples yellow, Ochre, Cadmium or Talens yellow

Reds: Burnt Sienna, Alizarin Crimson + Magenta or Rose Madder

Plein air tip: I chose a plain square palette because I do not hold my palette but rather wedge it in my tray. And just moving my paints around and searching for pigments, I made the mistake of putting my thumb through the hole. The wind caught the palette flipped my thumb back to my wrist which caused me extreme pain in the joint for the remainder of the week. Fortunately, it was my left hand, not my painting hand.

This particular combination works for me. You might need other colors as your base is due to your location on the globe. This palette works for earth tones and most of the vegetation around in Europe and North America. Tropical plants and climates may be radically different because of the type of vegetation which grows in these climates. However, when painting tropical plants have yet to find one which I wasn't covered in what I have outlined.

Three blues violet blue cast. Opaque French blue or cobalt blue the French blue is a an acceptable substitute in most cases for the more exotic and definitely more expensive cobalt blue. However, if you use cobalt blue, after you've acquired sufficient skilled to use it, you will notice that colors do not gray as much when mixed with cobalt blue. It is definitely the color of my preference.

All the mistakes committed by great artists are due to their having separated themselves from the truth, believing that their imagination is stronger... There is nothing stronger than nature. With nature in front of us we can do everything well." Seraglio quoted by Elton John V Perez Lougon, Le captain Sorolla E Lemal Tara the Huntington",

Heraldo de Madrid, 24 August 1915. Franco Francisco pond Sorolla, The Painter, Sorolla, Sotheby's publication, 1989

Examples:

Blue green cool cast translucent. Prussian blue. Prussian blue in the Old Holland paint is an extremely vibrant and tinctoral color. If you get it on your hand you will notice it everywhere. However, it is the color choice for many of the ocean blue greens. It mixes well with Naples yellow to make a silvery gray and blue greens you find in nature and it makes some fabulous pure greens with the cadmium yellow or Talens yellow, not to mention rich purples and violets of the sea.

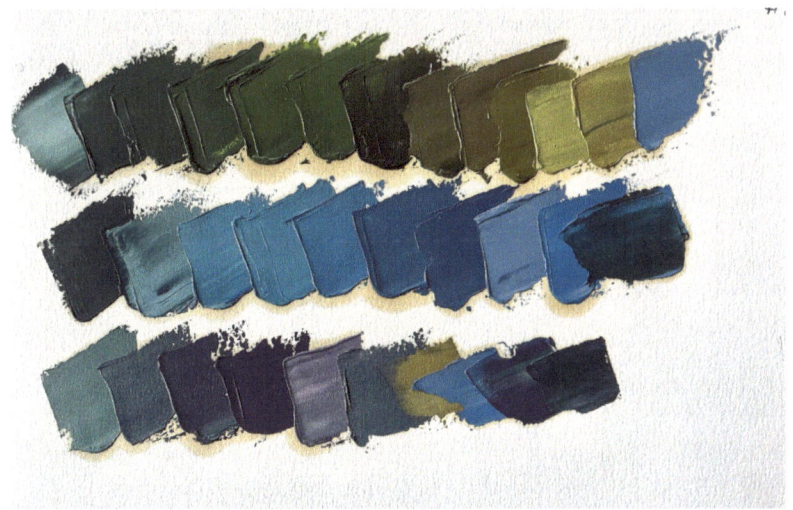

Yellow blue warm cast opaque Cerulean. Cerulean is the color most often associated with the sky. I use it in conjunction with the cobalt for that purpose. However you are in for a treat when you try mixing cerulean with a tinge

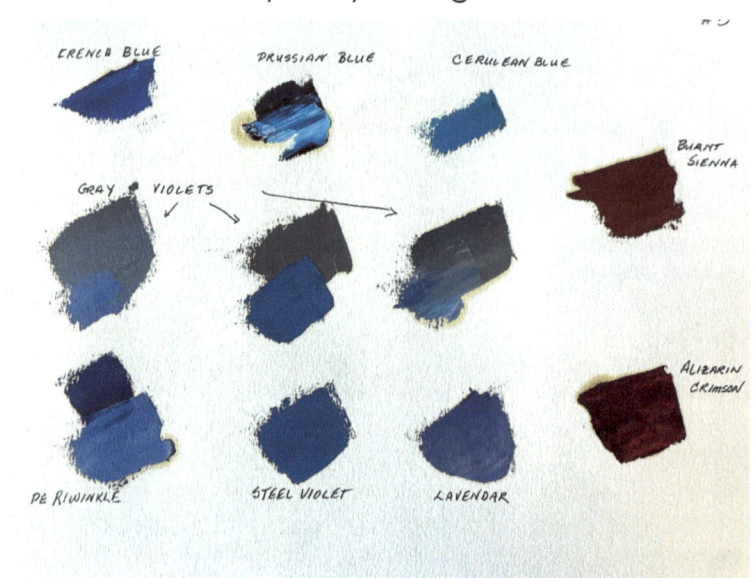

of Alizarin Crimson for interesting violet colors. Or mix it with the white and a tinge of Talens yellow for those sea foam greens you see in my marines. It can be beautiful color mixed with the right combinations.

3 yellows - pure yellows. Cadmium yellow or Talens yellow. I discovered Talens yellow, which is my preference, after a lot of searching. It is a color that mixes all the pure greens you need in nature, but also in great combination color with burnt sienna. You can mix those early spring greens, which are actually almost orange, with this color combination most people will swear that it is green.

Dull yellow opaque Naples. An instructor of mine once asked me why I had Naples yellow on the palette. He took my Ochre and mixed it with the white and said see! It is the same. This is just our secret OK? It isn't the same. Naples yellow is a color, for which I have found so many uses in nature that I say it is a basic to my color palette. Naples, mixed with almost any combination on the palette I've given you, will give you those unusual and bizarre grays of subtle rock colors, dirt and dust, flowering grasses and dead reeds... We'll get into that more or later in the exercise.

Earth tone opaque Ochre. A color with which to mix alternative greens; to make subtler contrast in flesh tones,; or contrast in a pig versus a translucent effect. It's mixes fabulously combinations with the burnt sienna, Naples to make a host of warm sand colors.

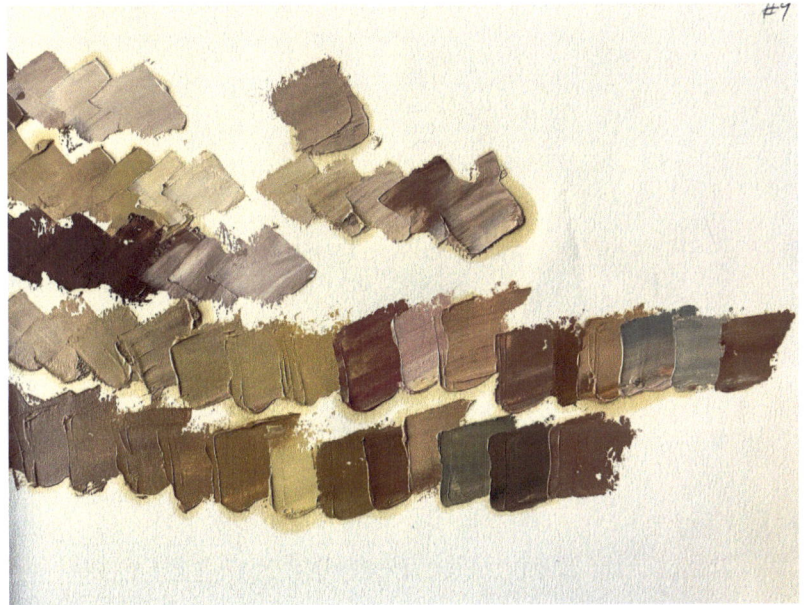

And two reds

Pure red translucent Alizarin Crimson. Alizarin Crimson is again one of the most powerful colors. A very little goes a long way. This color is a good basic red for almost all color mixing if you are painting some types of flowers you will need a magenta, which is a violet red. If you are painting poppies, you will need a cadmium red. Other than that, Alizarin Crimson will mix everything you could hope for in the sky earth plants and people.

Dull earth tone opaque Burnt Sienna. The burnt sienna of Old Holland is a beautiful sienna. It has a rose cast to it, which can emulate the pink granite in the sand, or it can be mixed with Naples to make beautiful coral colors. To make it orange cast you simply add a little Talens yellow. If you mix it with French blue you will have a beautiful Violet gray that can be used in your storm clouds or shadows on the road. You'll notice the one thing right away. There are both translucent and opaque colors in each of the primary categories. There is also brilliant and dull on my palette.

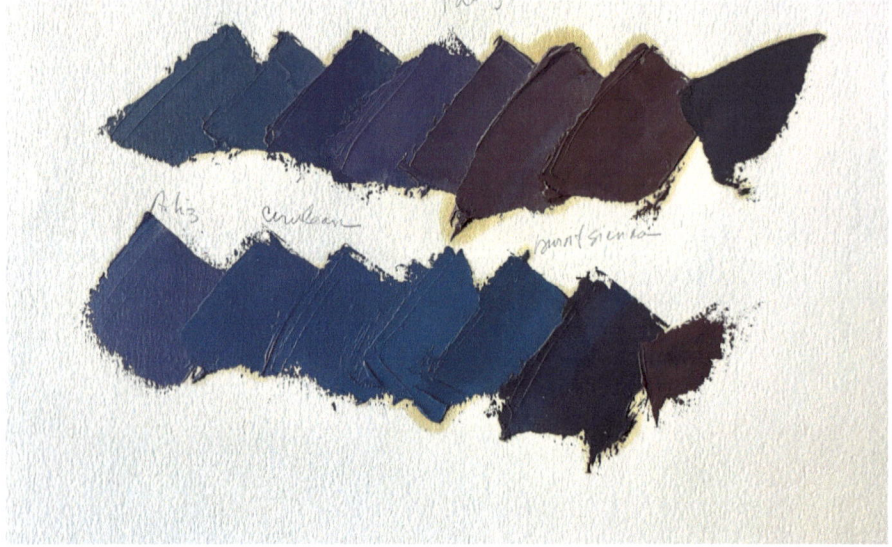

What I am doing is copying nature's habit of contrasting before ever mixing a color, that's ensuring that I am able to arrive at the desired colors after mixing. Also the colors which I have chosen are basic to the subjects.

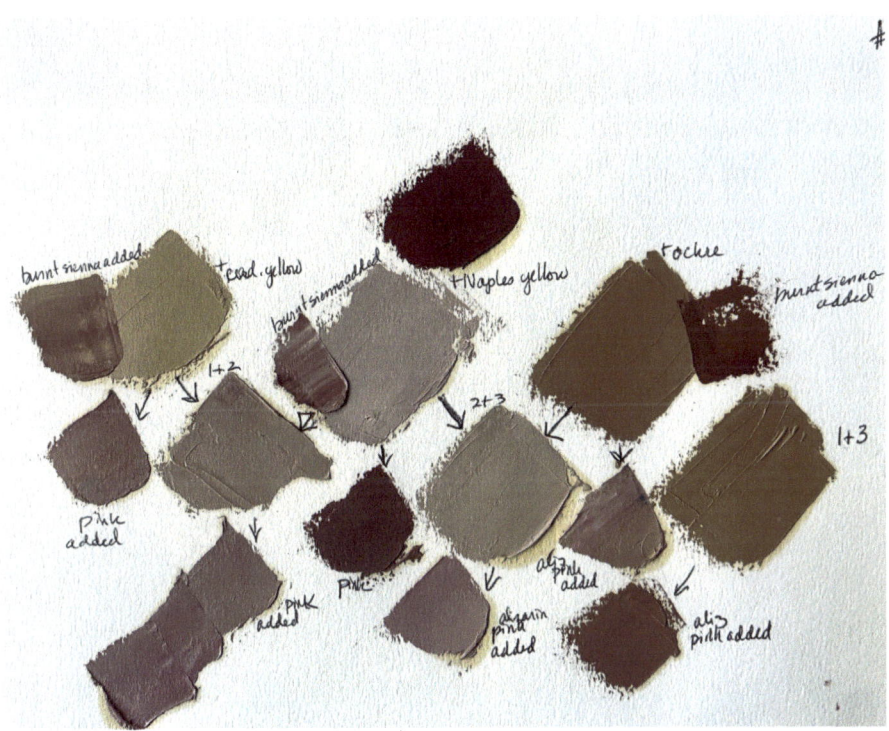

Mixing harmonious color

I've noticed that generally there are several ways to arrive at similar tones.

For example: if you mix in Naples yellow with Sienna depending on how much of each color you mix, you will arrive at your basic beach foundation color of coral pink. If you take Yellow Ochre and mix it with the Burnt Sienna, you arrive with a slightly different tone of coral pink. If you take your Cadmium Yellow and mix it with the Burnt Sienna again you arriving at a slightly different tone of coral pink. This seems relatively fundamental, it is surprising to me how few people understand this principle. If you choose a base color Burnt Sienna in this example and vary the other color in this example we vary the yellows you will find that you end up with a variety of colors all of which will harmonize. This works for any combination of color and makes it extremely easy to explore a host of tones and create variety.

Similarly, mix a batch of coral pink and divided up into four or five piles. Varied amounts of blues or reds added to each pile using your coral pink as your constant. You will end up with an unlimited range of colors, all of which will harmonize. The same would be true of green or any other combination you desire

***Trick of plein air painters of the past century;

If you study Courbet's landscapes/seascapes you will notice that he used beach colors in the sky and sky colors and the beach which enhanced and beautifully harmonized seascapes on the north coast of France during the last century. So you can use one part of the landscape to tie it to another, or gray down a color which will bring your painting together

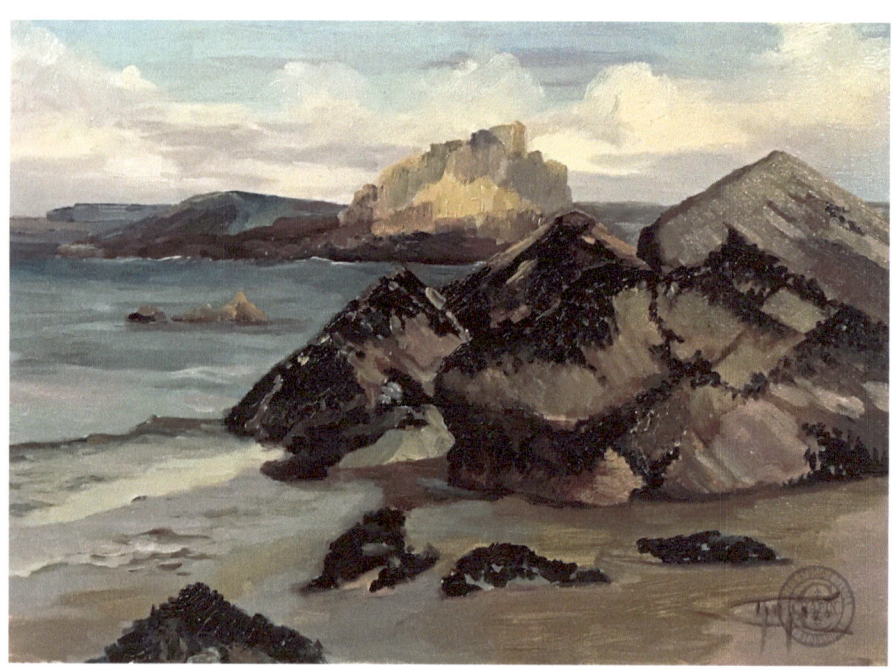

The whole problem with our contemporary art market, as I see it, is that our standards for professionalism have been too low. We have been missing the mark because we have been aiming at the wrong mark. Masters in plein air painting like Sorolla, Courbet, Homer... And all the women that have been ignored are the historical standards for this type of work. A contemporary artist is not a master artist despite publicity labels. A master artist, can only be determined by the historical sorting out That takes place at the end of an era or epoch. If we set our standards by comparison of our work to contemporaries, whose work has not been proven in historical context then our standards are open to question. This allows us to easily be misled by marketing interests.

You can do a study of plein air paintings by reading a book and certainly you will learn some things, but that is not what we are doing. Here we are trying to do a serious exploration, sort through the hype and word usage that is pushed at our profession. The aim is that we, who are professionals working in the field, become the determiners of what constitute good plein air painting and good plein air work versus those touted by the advertising marketing interest. The purpose of comparison is established standards set by recognize Masters and raise the caliber of our profession as a group.

Quote from Professional Plein Air Painters Discussion

May 28, 2000, Deborah Chapin

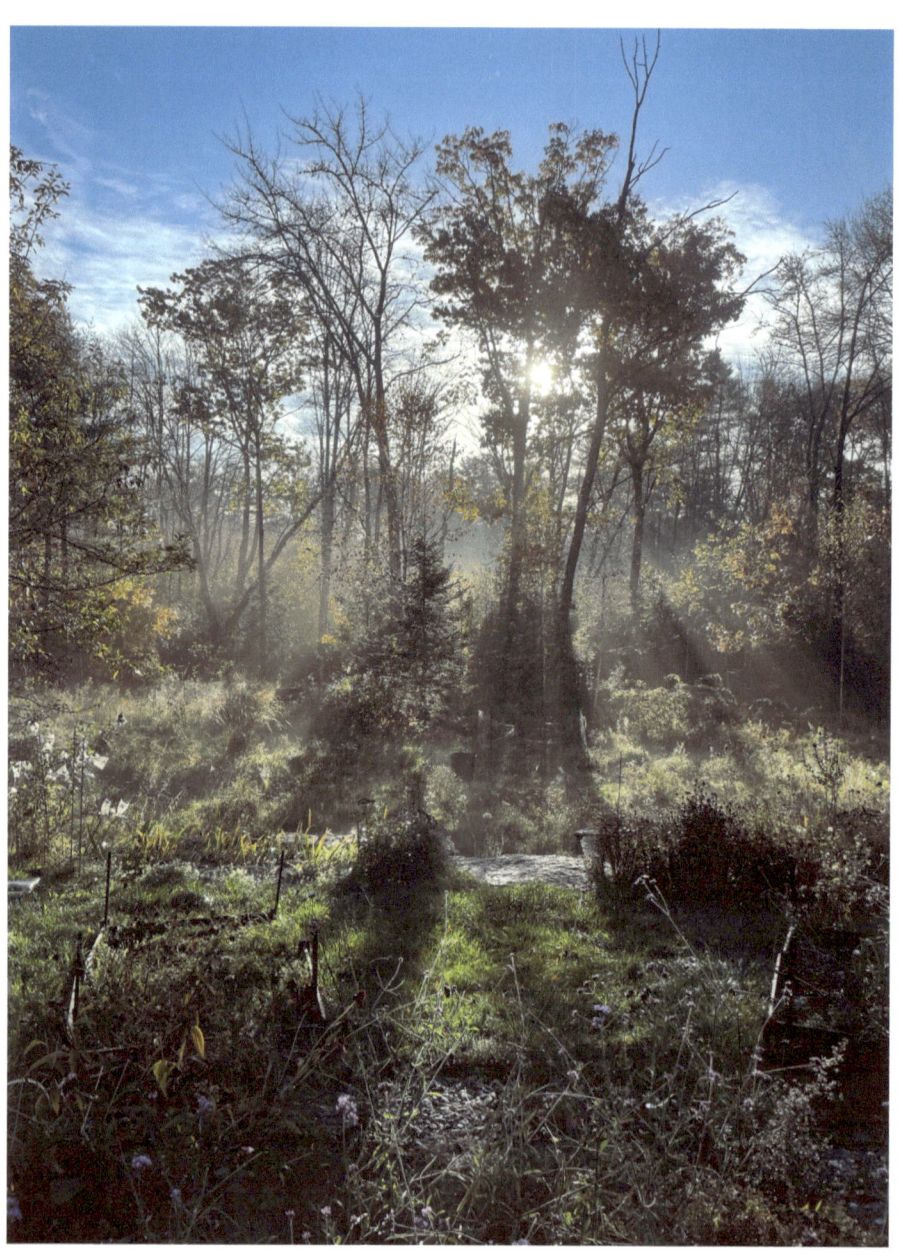

Nature's light

Light:

The most important consideration with this element is time. How long is it going to last? Light is an elusive factor in landscape For seascapes. Light is the color palette, and as such, can be used to create dramatically different affects on the same subject.

Also, light in conjunction with the Landscape or Seascape, can be used as a significant compositional element, and to my mind is more often than not is the compositional element.

Water, sky and sand all have significant reflective qualities and this, in conjunction with light, can be used to create spectacular color, light and dark patterns and hence, compositional patterns. Light is also dependent on the time of day, season of the year, location on the globe and weather. Light also does not rest and has a temperature or hue for relatively brief periods of time. I've found that, except for an overcast day, the light remains at the same temperature i.e. cold, cool, warm, hot for only a few hours at a time it is constantly on the move.

The different types of light:

There is **reflected light** and **back lighting** light which passes through an object **diffused lighting** and **refracted light**,

Time of day and seasons of the year will give you different light temperatures …Particular locations on the globe will give you different types of light dependent on the weather, humidity levels etc. The possibilities are endless. Even if you painted the same landscape over and over again, it would never be the same way twice.

Temperature gauge from dawn to late morning to afternoon to sunset

Let us limit ourselves to the different types of light and some examples of where one can find these particular types of lighting effects.

Morning Dawn	Early Morning	Mid-Day	Mid-Afternoon	Late-Afternoon	Evening Twilight
Cool Blue	Warming	Whitest	Warm White	Warm with red or orange	Cooling to Violets

Refracted light is the light, which passes through an object and the object bends the light or bounces it off the surface because of the objects form, such as a vase made of cut crystal or or a boat hull.

Back lighting light which passes from behind an object. The object can be translucent or opaque such as a building. Any type make for fascinating effects with the type of lighting which can be seen through such as glass or crystal translucent surfaces or water. Also, flower petals are often translucent, and back lit as are leaves on the trees, lace curtains, and the hair on someone's head.

Diffused light is the light that passes through an opaque object or surface such as a cloud and spreads the light in an even pattern this occurs on an overcast day and is the longest lasting lighting affect. This means you can paint as long as there is cloud cover. A lamp or opaque glass can also diffuse light such as in a light bulb. As the lighting effect in and of itself, however it is not this most interesting effect.

Reflected light is perhaps the most prevalent lighting effect in nature and the easiest to find. You have light bouncing all over the place; off the house onto a grass and vice versa off of boat onto the water and vice versa. Reflected light creates some very interesting lighting effects and combined with interesting colors lines and distortions, it can make your painting pop off the wall.

"Homer: "I prefer every time a picture composed and painted outdoors. The thing is done without your knowledge knowing it. Very much of the work now being done in studio should have been done in the open air. This making studies and then taking them home to use them it's only half right. You get composition but you lose freshness; you miss the subtle and to the artist, the finer characteristics of the scene is self". Homer interview by George Sheldon in "sketches and studies", art journal, NS6 1880, PP 107 - 108.

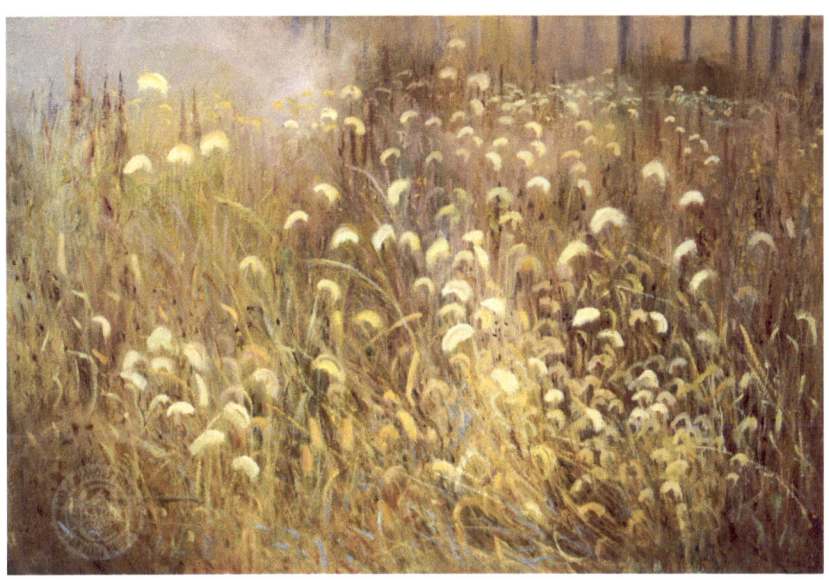

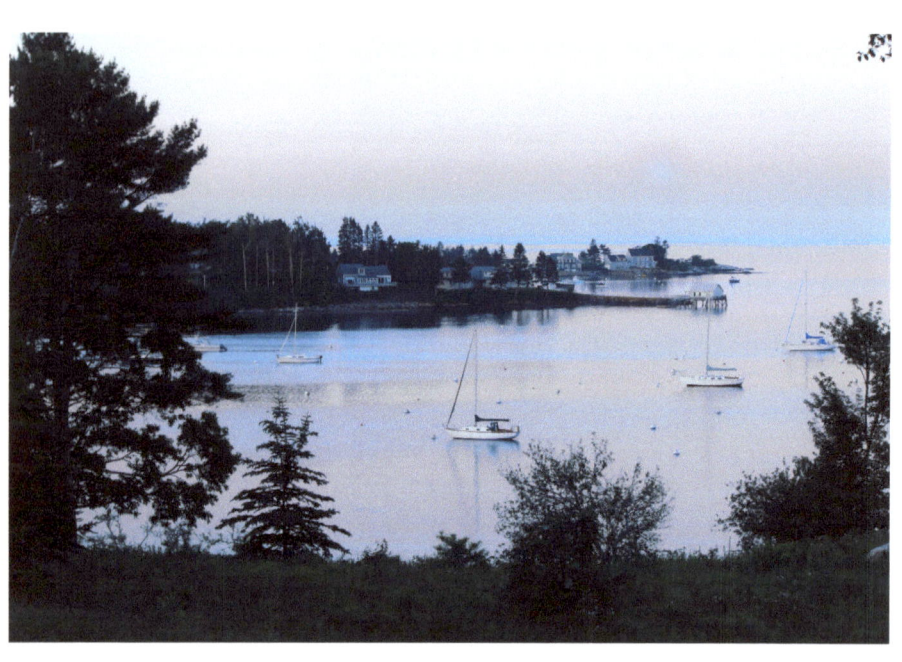

Nature's line

Line is one of the main elements, which suggests movement. Line, which is static such as the horizontal line in the horizon, indicate stability and rest. Lines such as diagonals and zigzags imply unsettling elements and so create momentum. With momentum comes movement.

Composition and line are intimately associated. My definition of composition composition is the division of space that's it! Anytime you draw a line you are dividing a space. Space can be divided up in myriad of ways, all of which are legitimate, but some make direction direct references back to nature and some are more interesting than others.

- By dividing up the space, using the basics of perspective i.e. lines converging to a point on the horizon, you create a three-dimensional feel based on those experiences of seeing in reality. For example, a road disappearing into the distance.

- One could divide the space in on the canvas into thirds, 2/3 can be either sky or land, but the main divisions line of the landscape is the horizontal line.

- Conversely, if you want to does the stabilize the experience of the viewer, take the horizon line away from the viewer all together, creating uncertainty by losing the normal visual reference.

- If you want to create the feeling of dynamics or imbalance, search for the landscape or seascapes with diagonal lines.

- The most important lines, to the artist who wants to paint movement, are the curved in the serpentine lines.

Using lines of light form or color to divide space.

- Lines of light This is one of my favorite elements of composition in landscape of Seascape. Watching the shadows of clouds pass over field and divide up the landscape, or a hillside, or ocean into spaces of light and dark, seeing how that affect the color, can be a thrilling thing to observe. One is sometimes tempted to forget to paint and just watch the drama unfold. But don't do that. Picking up the shadow patterns which best suits your subject, creates impact on the scene. It can be used to emphasize or D emphasize elements within the piece. It's a tremendously fluid tool and the artist can use it to its best advantage.Lines of color; where the sea meets the rocky sure is a line of color. Where the sky meets the tree line of a hillside, that's a line of color. A reflection play upon the pond, that's a line of color. These are most often dramatic contrast of color by eat cool against warm, as in the sea and the rocky shore, or most active line against the static in the reflection. Therefore, use it wisely. If your color harmony doesn't work and your composition is off or your line is a beautiful is going to show up dramatically in these instances.

- Lines of form form is the least utilized element in the painting today. Perhaps it's because too few really can draw in form requires the ability to draw well. When you see a silhouette a tree against a brilliant sky, that's form Must be exquisite or the whole painting will fail. If you have trouble with forms and need to work on their execution, then put the paint down and draw. Draw it until it looks as beautiful as the form. Then go back to paint.

Since this discussion is primarily geared to those who are already conversant in composition we will not go into detail discussion of composition here for reference please see the suggested readings in the bibliography.

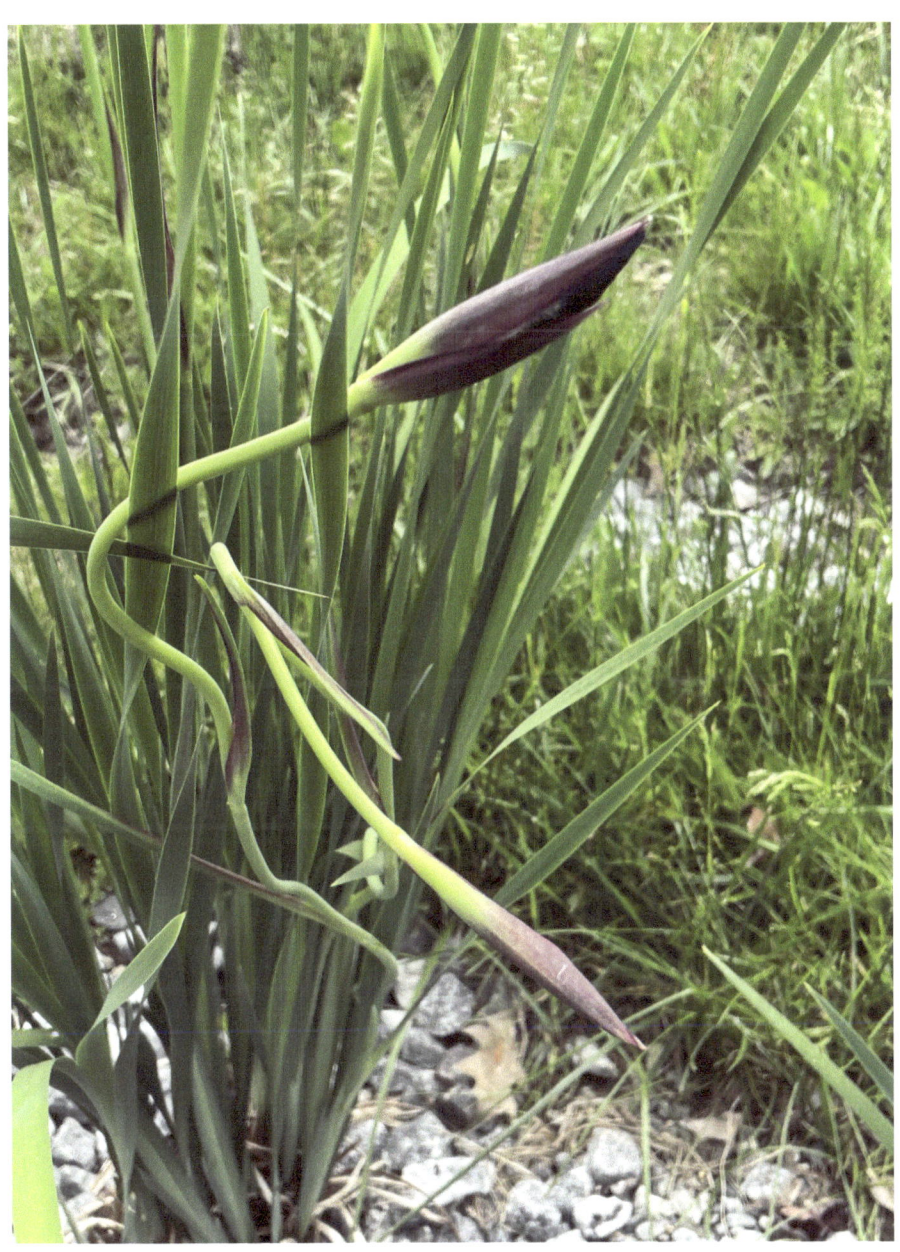

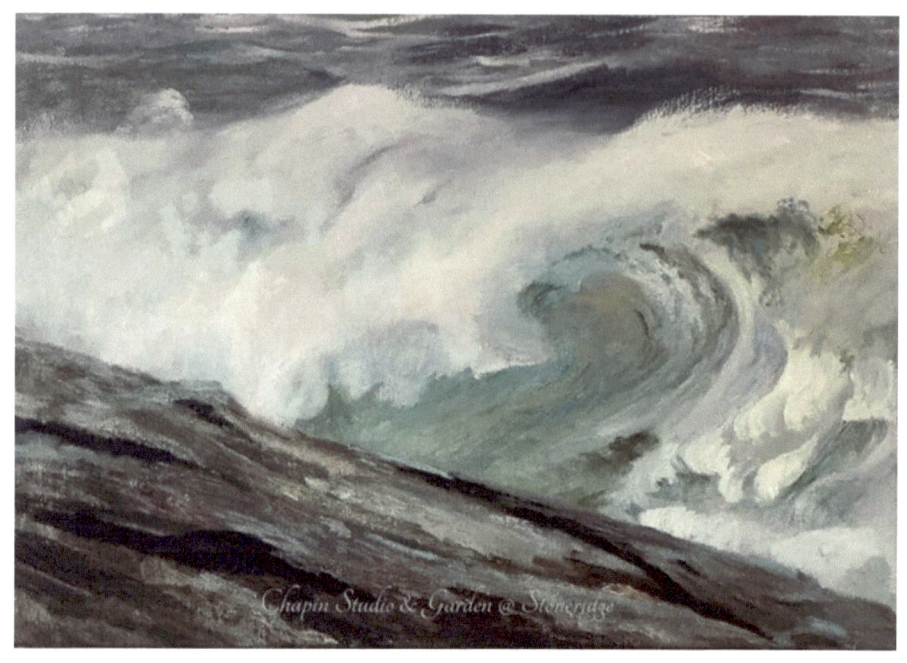

See White Horses videos

Life and movement - Seeing It.

- **Color and light capturing transient effects**. How it affects your subjects and how to use it.

As we discussed in the chapter on natures like your colors are affected by the Time of day during which you are painting. In the early morning your colors may be cooler than your if you painted the same scene later in the afternoon or evening. So if you are contrasting warm and cool colors and your subject is warm colored, paint early in the Day to maximize that effect. If you want to paint a subject that consistently is mainly a cool color and you want to warm them up paint them in the evening. If you want to emphasize the cool aspect, paying a cool subject in the morning. If you want to dazzle with warm colors paint the warm subjects in the afternoon or evening. Likewise, if your main emphasis is a brilliant lighting affect the sun is brightest at the high noon. Buy thinking just a little about your subject, you will enhance your results.

- **Repetitive movement:** capturing a movements gesture by seeing the repetitions.

Nature repeats herself as do people. We see patterns of movement, just like seasons of the year, if we start looking for them. You can capture of moving subject by dividing up the movements and departs, as I discussed in the sea skipping figurative examples of chapter 6. Look for repetitions, these can be successfully and rendered on plein air.

- **Creating wind movement and changing weather affects**

Wind movement, clouds in their accompanying lines, most often depicting changeable weather patterns. We associate clouds with the coming and going of climate changes and the shadows that they cast as indicators of their passing. Clouds are really vapors and fluff, soft edges and like capturing elements. They have formed like everything else, with lights and darks, just like painting an apple or a pear but their edges are generally less defined. Loose is better when it comes to clouds and getting to the feel of any particular type of cloud comes with practice.

- **Creating moving lines and apparently still subjects**

As discussed in <u>Nature's Line</u> and the <u>Chapter on Finding Design</u>, you will see how you can create movement even in apparently still subjects by looking for serpentine and curve lines and emphasizing directional flow.

<u>Meanders of the Sea XIII</u>

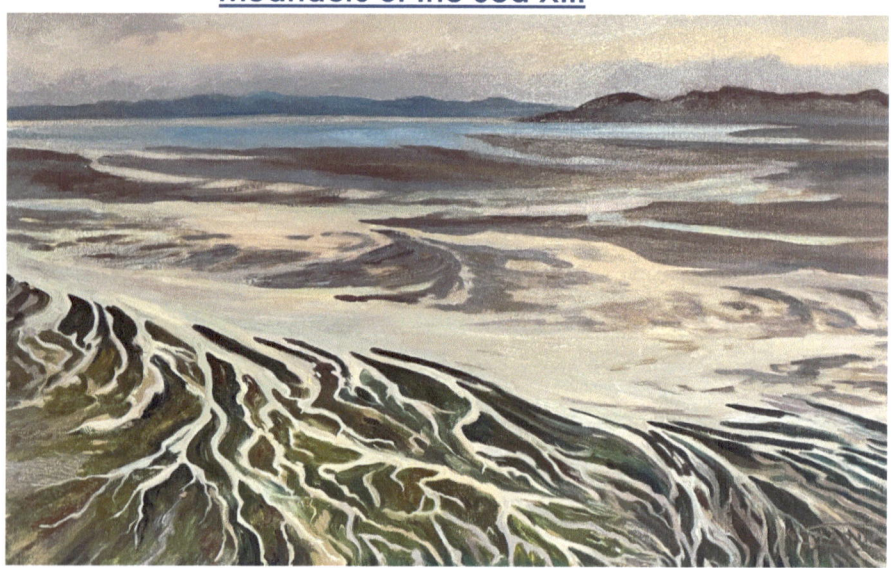

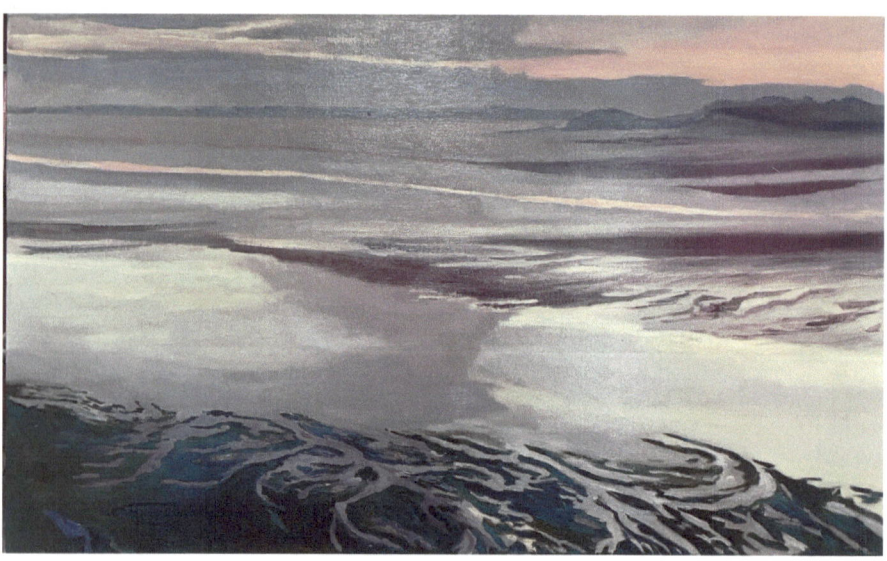

Picking a Subject

- **Ideas to consider when choosing a subject:**

Everyone has her own way of deciding what she wants to paint. My primary focus, and I believe my most successful paintings, or results of searching for and finding strong designs combined with beautiful color. Many factors play a role in this but those are the two Allen's her which I search. When I find them in rich abundance I produce well.

- **Recognizing the beautiful piece in raw form.**

It is obvious that a subject will make a beautiful painting since the subject is spectacular. However, one of the more challenging aspect sister recognize a beautiful spot with loads of potential when it isn't particularly and it's prime. I look for the design aspects and then break it down in stages. Each aspect must answer a question with an affirmative to some degree. Below is my checklist of ideas I run through when choosing a spot.

- **Questions to ask:**

1. Is there a strong design element in the scene?

2. Is it accessible?

3. What might it look like in different lights?

4. Gazing at the subject for 15 to 20 minutes do some things start to reveal themselves?

5. Are there subtleties with which I can play?

6. How many interesting elements can I find in this spot to put into the piece?

7. Is it a one painting spot or are there potentially many paintings here?

I'm careful with my selections of painting material. Some people believe that you can paint anything and it will be beautiful, however, if this is the case then I think how much more can be accomplished with the carefully chosen subject.

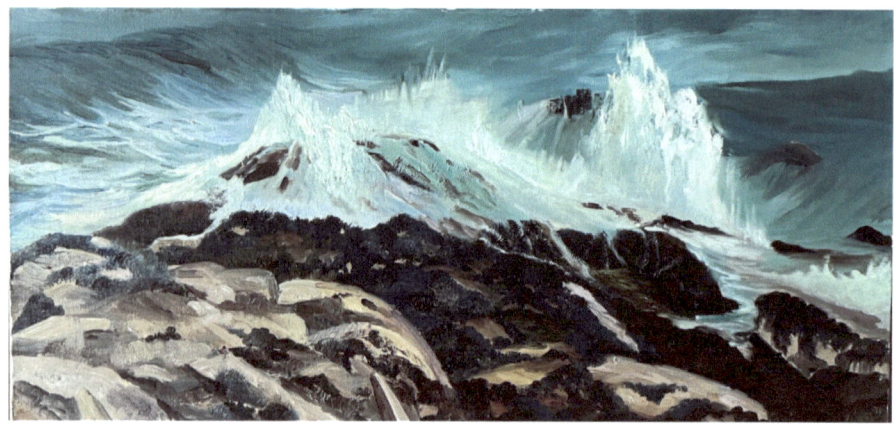

Developing a Plan of Attack

The key is research. Preparation is through the experience of viewing your subject in all sorts of lights and conditions, will be your best aid. Some say that I am too calculating in my approach. Yet I have seen spots that were begging to be painted. I am quite capable of being spontaneous. I found that I couldn't rely on serendipity as a basis for a career. To increase the odds of successful painting on plein air, for the long-haul, research and preparation's are important. Planning, in conjunction with tide, light, seasons of the year, etc. have yielded some of my best paintings

Pieces like a passing cloud on the cover can only be found in caption with preparation, planning and experience. Wiggling it down bit by bit and solving each problem or obstacle as it comes along. Also it can only be accomplished by repeatedly painting the same subject.

Preparation for the predictable lighting effects and timing its use in my work. I'd like to see the same subject in the different lights. With experience, I have gained a certain sense of what may be beautiful at a certain time of day or with a certain effect influencing it. I search for the particular combination of light, and color and composition, which will make a spectacular statement or render a quiet beauty.

Preparation of color and palette in advance. I don't mix all of my colors in advance of setting up. When I start a piece I do mix a predominant color theme for blocking in large masses. I always have my palate ready to go. Nothing is more frustrating than settling setting up an easel and being prepared to start a piece and then finding there is not enough white or on the palette.Preparation work to capture the moving subject. Preparing to paint something that is moving takes ......such as a figure or the ocean, requires Special preparation. You can't get practice without attempting and failing. Support of the successful piece encompasses a myriad of not so successful previous efforts. If you are totally successful in all painting, you are doing one of two things deluding yourself or formula painting. You should be Moving up to new Challenges.Different subjects but the same overall plan of attack a checklist. Now that you have a subject before you. How are you going to capture it on your canvas? Here are some guidelines to help you develop your subject. Whether you were painting irises in the garden or rolling waves on the rocky cliff these are will help you succeed.

In planning the time of day to use all the predictive skills which you discussed in the chapter in preparation for the field and select it is subject and its location

1. Look at the subject and study as major movement pattern lines

2. Mix a batch of color contained in that major movement line or pattern you wish to lay in

3. Draw in the major movement lines and then the secondary movement lines

4. Paint in the subject using the movement lines as your guide for directions of brush work and continue until you have all your foundation painting in.

5. Painting details, highlights and deepest darks at the end. Retaining the movement lines and colors you originally saw as you are lead in paint.

Some people like to paint the deepest darks in at the beginning and sometimes so do I. I find this to be less fluid method of working and more restrictive. Painting with the range of color values from the beginning gives you the greatest mobility in paint; helping develop a painting; and keeps you from making mistakes in value, form and color. This means you have a chance to judge and adjust your painting at the beginning what it is of the crudest and save the highlights and deepest darks until the end of the painting. If the painting works well without the deepest darks in the brightest highlights then when these will make the final piece shine.

" When I begin thinking of most valuable assets I have as an artist I came to the conclusion that being able to come up with ideas, my observation abilities, my imagination, being all able to dream and knowing my sources of inspiration were at the top of the list. I thought that if I could discern the process by which I arrived at these assets, I could repeat the process more often and does achieve a higher level of creativity and productivity in my artwork. Developing creative Powers by Deborah Chapin

Brushwork the Interpreter of Movement

People don't realize what an amazing thing you're mind is doing when painting en plein air. You will see all sorts of Brushwork in your piece, which is an immediate translation of your environment directly from your mind, through your hand, onto the canvas. This is the forte of oils. You can record this interaction; this is the often misunderstood world of Brushwork.

Seeing brushwork and how brushwork describes the speed direction and spirit of movement. Brushwork is the main means of expression of the direction speed and spirit of the interaction between the artist in the subject. Brushwork Is the Chef d'orchestra leading this interpretation of movement, light and color. It is the Brushwork, which tells of you what the main reason or impetus behind the expression in paint is and the source of inspiration behind the piece. Without good brushwork your painting will be flat and under interesting.

How do use the Brushwork to interpret movement: start with the idea that the brushwork is the interpreter of movement. What is it you wish to portray? Is it a sweeping motion of the clouds, or a splaying of the grass by the wind, or the dancing movement of a leaf falling to the ground? Think in these terms. Imitate the sweeping movements with your hand. Portray the moving cloud or a flickering dancing leave.

How to interpret the direction of movement. Discovered the direction in which the object is moving. Is the wind sashaying the wind back-and-forth? Interpret that movement with a hand by sashaying the brush back-and-forth. Is the movement of directional line such as that of a wave surging into the shore? Follow the movement with your brush. Starting at the origin of the moment too it's sweeping conclusion, with one long brushstroke. Exaggerate the movement with your arms just like the dancer exaggerates the line in the hands by extending the arm.

How to Portray Speed. The speed of application should match the speed of the movement. Your brushes speed depends on a certain resistance factor of the canvas. This is why I like to do a scrubbing in of shapes divided up the canvas into tonal shapes. When you see a peaceful scene in which time is allowed to dally during the painting of the piece, you'll see that the brushwork is more sedate. If you are painting active surf however, the speed of application and the amount of paint use in order to convey the subject will result in a vigorous brush work. This is matching your brushwork to your subject.

The brush work depicting old trees for example would differ from that of an active marine where you would want to create wet and active effects. Let the brush work help describe the activity of the scene.

The Touch. The touch makes a difference. Powerful movements need powerful brushstrokes, and forceful application of pain. It takes energy to translate energy. Delicate sensitive sentiments need a light touch, with brush just grazing the surface of the canvas or previously applied paint.

Holding the Brush: Likewise, holding the brush in different ways gives you better brush control and improve sensibility of touch. Holding it as an extension of your thumb over your hand can be used to tremendous advantage to sketch. Holding a large brush at arms length to give you those sweeping movements grace and power. Choking up on the brush can be used to scrub in your areas of color.

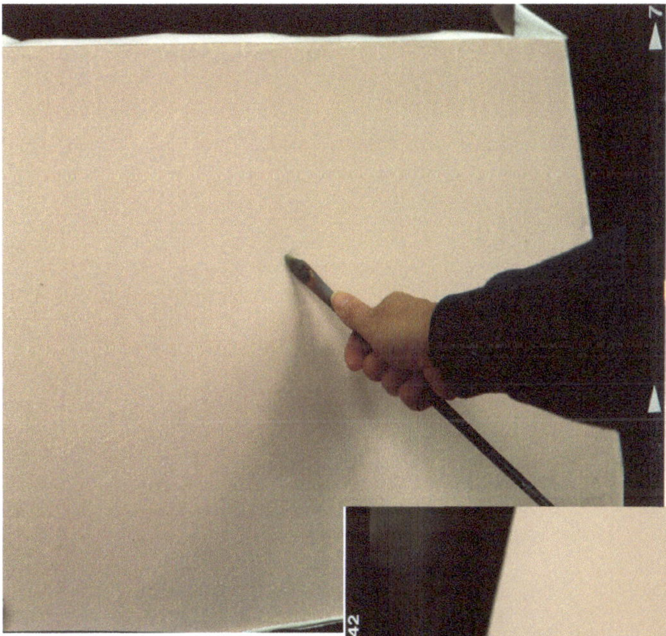

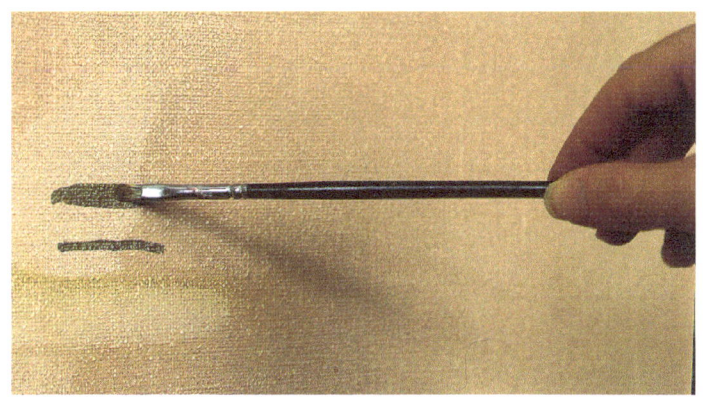

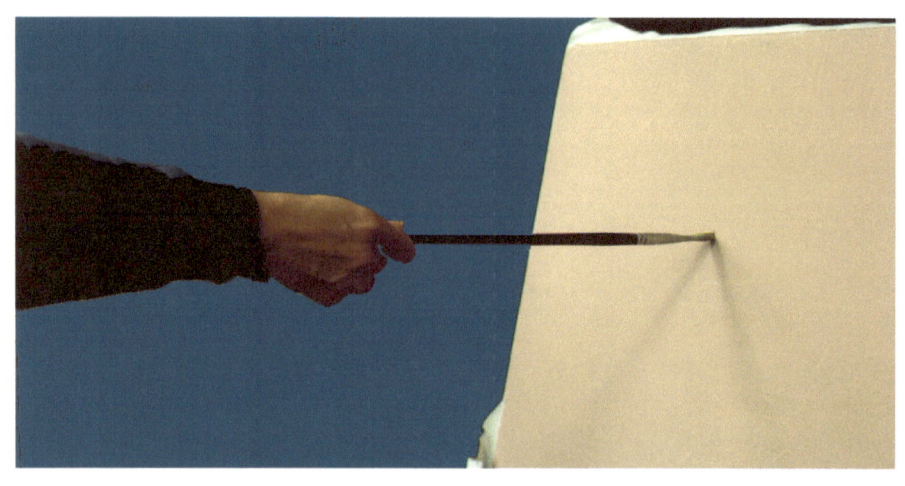

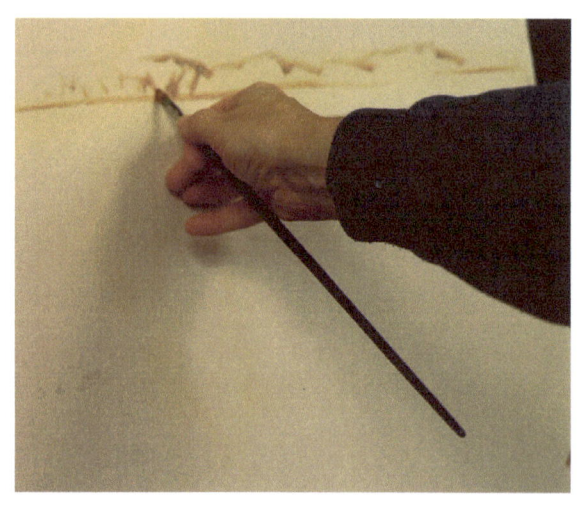

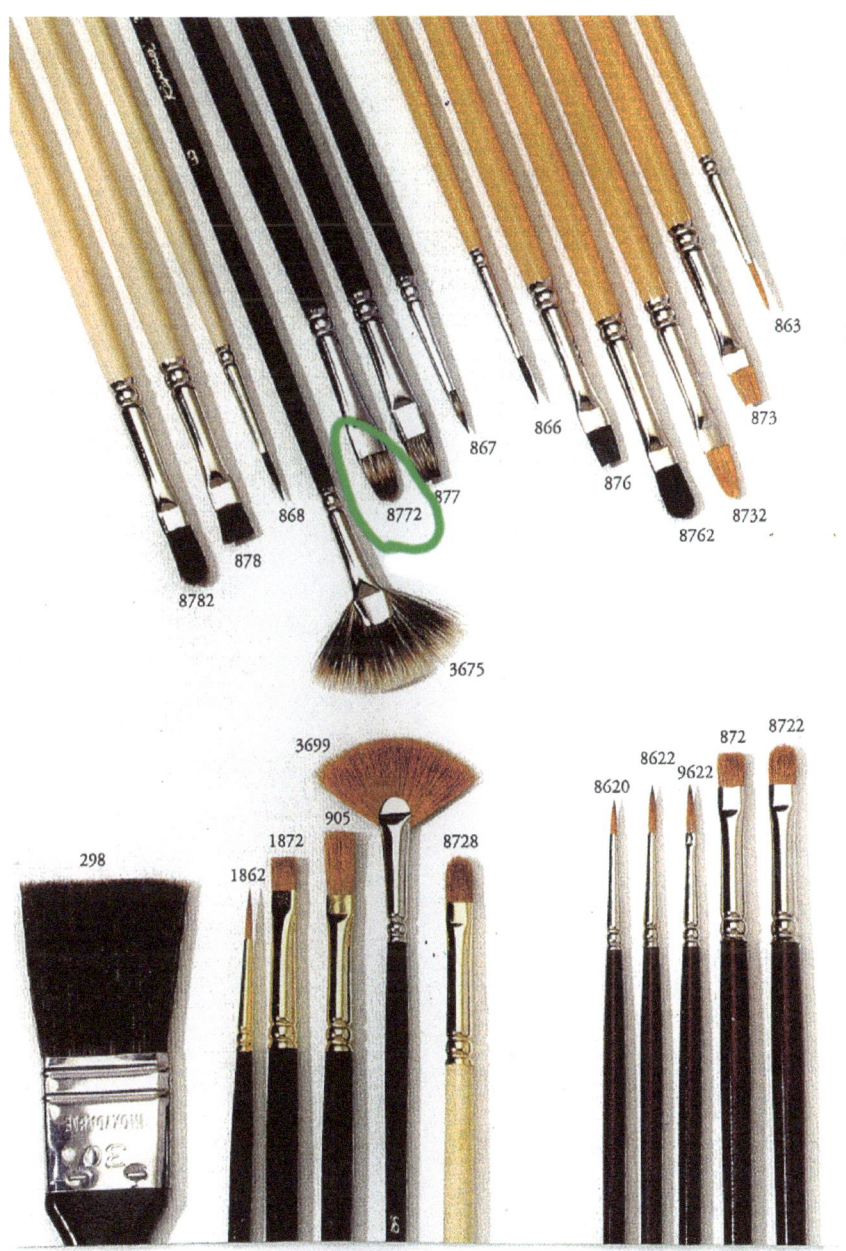

863

873

867

866

868

8772

877

876

878

8732

8782

8762

3675

3699

872

8722

905

8622

9622

1872

8728

8620

298

1862

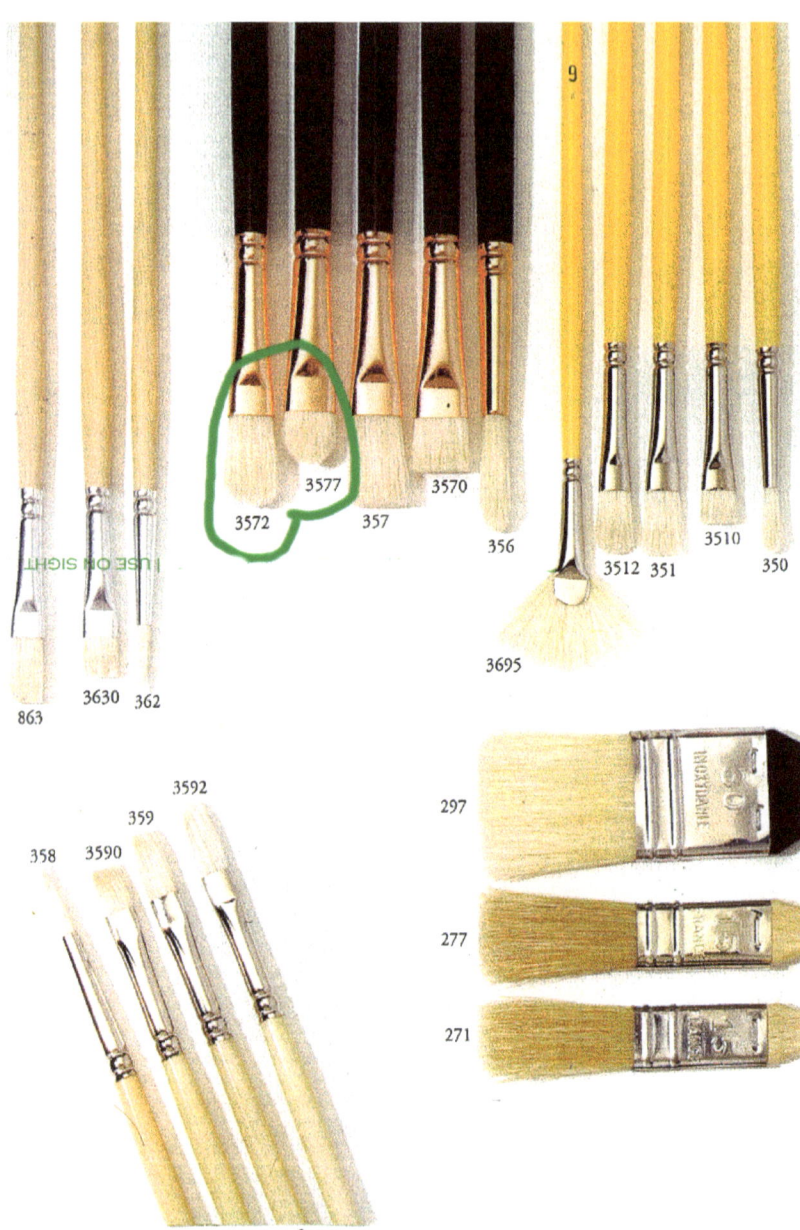

I USE ON SIGHT

3577

3572   357   3570

356

3512 351

3510

350

3695

297

277

271

863   3630 362

358 3590   359   3592

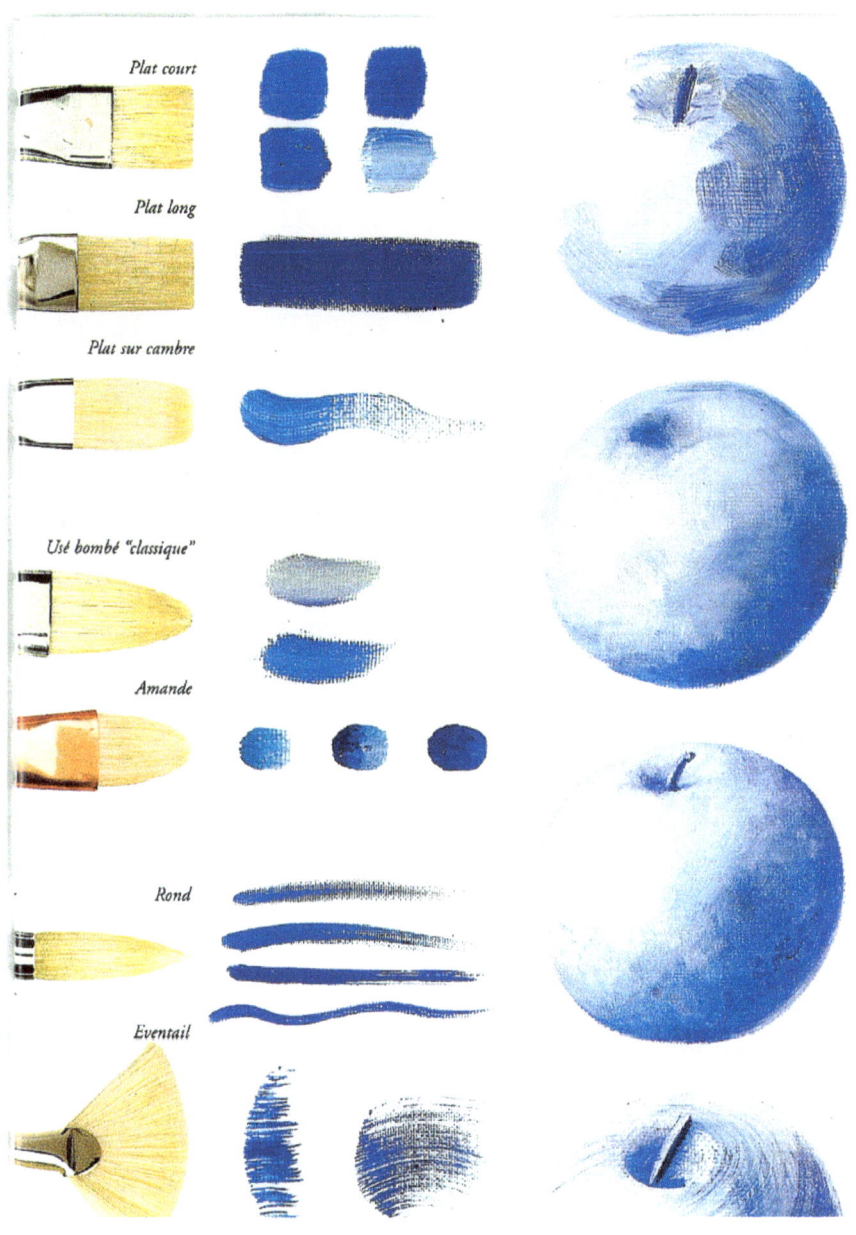

Plat court

Plat long

Plat sur cambre

Usé bombé "classique"

Amande

Rond

Eventail

How much paint to put on your brush. This is a singularly important factor and how are you brushwork will look. Getting the right amount of paint for your purpose can only come with experience. But generally I work more impasto or with more pain with active brushwork I like smooth areas such as sound or to looks more smooth so I might minimize the Brushwork by scrubbing in color, as described previously, and then overlaying texture for things which might sit on top of the sand. The rocks, which are rough, might be better depicted with more paint thereby giving them more textural solidity.

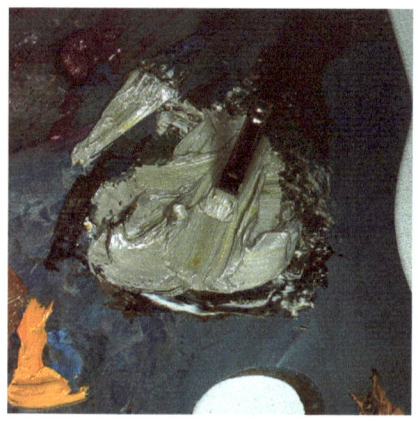

Making the brushwork work to your advantage. We live in an age in which everything is glossed over, i.e. photography, TV, magazine ads, etc. However, oils have their own nature, which can be used to tremendous advantage to capture scenes has no other medium can do. So use it and don't try to hide it! Look at how all the grades in plein air painting used it. Look at homers seascapes Sorolla's beach scene sergeants beach portraits Corbet's landscapes in seascapes. Even the brushwork of Rembrandt's portraitures has an impressionistic feel to it. One in brushstroke to indicate the finger, one for each joint Etc.

How to recognize good brush work in plein air paintings of others. If you view excellent plein air paintings you will begin to understand the Brushwork. You will see directional speed of line, and design all wrapped in luscious color and texture. Flickers of Brushwork remain seemingly randomly placed, are all the pieces of a puzzle and makes sense within the hole of the painting. It is not idle or careless dobbing of paint and as my instructor told me when I was starting out,"You are not painting a door". Like good color, it is distinctive and will be easy to recognize after a time. You will be privy to a secret world of the mind of the great artists, seeing their thoughts, their inspiration, and hearing them speak on canvas. Good brush work is not a slathering on of paint. That, is canvas daubed as Cole says "by people of weak intellect", who are more interested in emphasizing the brushwork over the subject or idea presented by the piece. Actually, they have no idea what they are doing. Go to the museums to see real Brushwork. You'll see the difference. You will also know who paints from photographs or by formula and who is really painting on site, in tune with the subject.

Summing up.

- A textural quality to the Brushwork. It should be three-dimensional and you should see it not necessarily overtly.

- It should look spontaneous and playful in spots.

- The speed of the movement of the brush and the direction of the Brushwork should match that of the subject in the movement of the piece.

- Color and Brushwork, as well as line, should have a harmonious feel.

- Nothing should be labored, artificial looking or contrived.

Knowing your purpose for painting can help you give your art direction and stimulate your creative energies. It is my opinion, that arts purpose visual fine art no longer includes depicting historical events, or re-creating world disasters. In this era we have other media which depicts these things in more relevant manner than the visual arts. World events have been taken over by film and journalistic writing. They have taken over this role because they are more fluid and in the world his pace is far faster than ever ancestors, this is important. I think that the role of art has been redefine. Art's main purpose is to inspire. Secondly, it is a main medium for depicting and capturing the soul of beauty in the world around us. There is no other media that does this as well.

Developing creative Powers by Deborah Chapin

Finding designs

Finding and using moving lines in apparent static subjects creates interest to your piece.

Look for serpentine lines, swooping and curves. These lines all suggest movement and will create momentum even in a static subject.

- **Using light shadow and color to suggest movement and moving lines.**

Let us use an example to create a project from scratch. The sea is a rich source of abstract design elements because it is fluid and not restricted by anything except a form into which it flows. The artist knows that it is generally easier to reach a beach soon so one has the possibility of completing a large work containing more design elements. The subject selected may be more complex in design and detail, if the wind is relatively light and the day is overcast so that the lighting remains constant. Although the beach may eventually be covered up by an incoming tide, and there are definitely the tourist to worry about, the limitations are fewer in doing a work of this kind. So let's discuss discuss an example of one of my favorite beaches. what are the major elements? Sand, Sea, sky and Rocks. If I plan to paint in the morning, what temperature will the light be? Cool. If it's partly cloudy how is that going to affect the Seascape? The color cools down when the clouds block out the light and by contrast emphasizes the warmth of the color when the light breaks through and hits the beach or water. when the land is cloaked in warm color, the sea becomes the cooler color. Additionally, when the sea turns gray tones in the major elements such as the sea in the sand, she then uses brilliant colors in the details such as the muscle stool violet on the rocks and the seaweed rust on the sand. You'll notice also that I haven't use the word gray until now to describe the mixing of color because too many people think that means adding black and white to your color. This is not what nature uses. See the discussion on natures color. There are neither blacks nor pure whites in nature. All these factors are considerations before you begin painting. Now search for ways to accent design.

When you see a cloud shadow overlay in your subject, which is one of the main ways of difference in light and shadow in the landscape or Seascape, you can use them to your advantage. They create serpentine or diagonal lines of color, light and dark to an add dimension of movement to your subject. If you see bright colors versus subtle colors you can use them to create moving lines apart from the subject itself. This is what I call "composition overlay by composition" or "design within design" Which makes for a fascinating piece. Most people don't even realize that they are using this technique

The difficulty of painting the sea is that you either get it or you don't, there are no second chances.

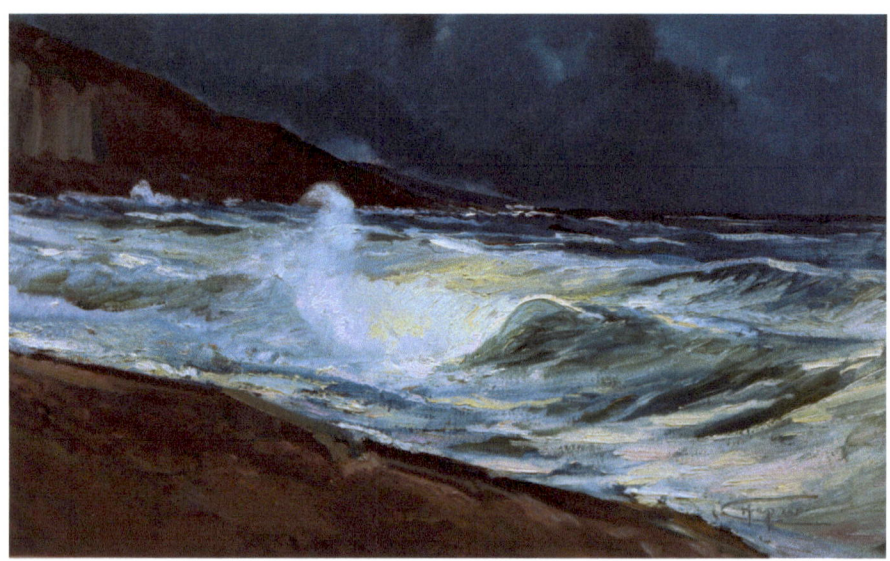

More Complex Subjects in Motion

Putting it all together to create powerful effect: (An approach to painting it.)

With painting more complex subjects, such as the sea or moving figure, the first step prior to painting is to study the subject. Whatever it takes to understand movement in any complex subject is critical for painting it well. The seas basic property is liquidity. The basic property of liquid is that it can assume any form and move in any direction without constraint. So be prepared to paint unfamiliar forms and let your preconceived ideas go. To capture particular water movement, it is helpful to study how it reacts to the land forming the coast where you are painting. Once you understand water, you can then tackle the subject of Coastal and use the same process you would use in paintings relatively simple subjects such as wheat field in the wind. The difficulty of painting the sea is that you either get it or you don't there are no second chances.

Here's a checklist I analyzed for the painting <u>Blue Indigo</u> successfully.

1. In painting a surf piece such as Blue Indigo I avoided depicting the rocks or background until the end, just scrubbed in a place holder in the predominant tones there.

2. Concentrate on the waves, which are the most transitory aspects of the painting.

3. Try to see the simple, constant rhythms and forms within the complex and impermanence scene.

4. Forget the crest of the wave is a wave at all

5. Concentrate on a specific time when the wave is cresting and disregard any other moment.

6. The crest line becomes a reference point.

7. Focus on painting one moment in time instead of millions of different ones. Establishing a timing element for

capturing movement in the key to observing, understanding, and painting a Seascape.

8. Once you have a reference point, move onto the larger shapes in the scene.

9. Study the wave and wait for it to approximate the line already placed on the canvas.

10. When the same wave action comes again, shift your attention from the crest line to the underlying colors of the wave painting simply and directly from lights to darks. (*Note: This is assuming you also have scrubbed in your patterns with the predominate light or dark under painting.)

You will also find out when the land is cloaked in cool colors the sea becomes the warmer color and vice versa.

The next shape to scrutinize is the curl of the wave, the part that is most turbulent.

1. Wait for the crest line, using that as a guide and waiting for it to resemble the initial one on your canvas. Then with vigorous brushstrokes, follow the movement of the curl, letting the top color again mix with the underlying colors. The key here is to emphasize the subject and not the process of painting.

2. Employing broad, horizontal cause strokes, render the shapes of the foam as a large mass of various shades of white with holes of green blue and yellow ochre.

3. To keep the colors as clean as possible use three or four brushes with whites and another three or four brushes for each additional color.

4. Finally paint the solid, stable rocks, background and sky.

5. After the foundation is intact, you're ready for those subtler details such as craggy facades of rocks seaweed flashes of light on the ocean surface etc.

6. Back in the studio tweak your piece, which is a refinement of shapes colors brushwork and even some

details. But be careful not to destroy your plein air brushwork.

- **Demonstration of the figure: an approach to painting on site**

I find that people move faster than the ocean. The ocean does repeated rhythmic motion so you can look for similarities. This is what you have to do with the moving figure. Learning the repetitions gives you an advantage.

1. I like to draw first the structure and position of the moving figure when using the model as a reference for color and shadowing. That I capture the feeling of the figure at the moment.

2. Work on a sketch in pencil on full paper for full scenes, and then improve on the sketch for overlaying tracing paper to give you a quick way to improve your pose or figure. Then trace the figure directly on canvas using a pastel with a composition which you've laid out **or** you can sketch your figure directly onto canvas and work from there. Advantage to drawing on papers that you also end up with a finished drawing and you may find a better pose along the way or refine your painting. This Takes more time so you might want to just do some sketching one day then come back and do a complete painting with figures on a different day. Lots of ways to approach it.

Note: I approach each subject and each day as a unique experience. I do not standardize how I do things because that doesn't allow me the sensitivity to the moment and subject. Otherwise you are just a an assembly manufacturer working on a line.

Each artist develop some manner of sketching of selecting, composing or painting that suits his (her) temperament, yet nearly all take advantage of artistic license. They generally express the main idea in a broad comprehensive way without sacrificing artistic quality to nature. Nor does nature need to be sacrificed to artistic purpose. There is no reason why the characteristics of a particular object should be lost by slight alterations of his contour, portion or some modification of his value, color or the changing of his (her) location.

Outdoor composition by Edgar Payne

Additional Video Explanations

- **Explanation of Tone & Aerial Perspective**
  https://vimeo.com/457230857

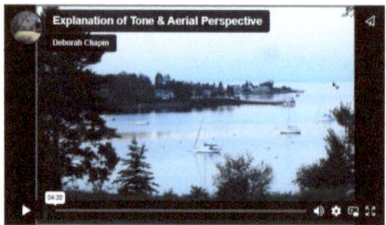

- **Demonstration Starting a Drawing of Rocks**
  https://vimeo.com/456774194

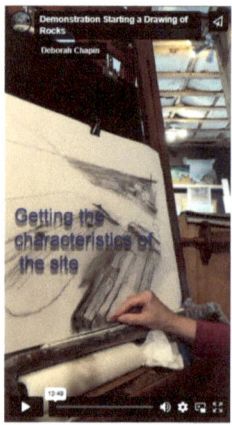

- **Perspective Practice House in snow**
  https://vimeo.com/454132651

- **Pemaquid Harbor House**
  https://vimeo.com/457048137

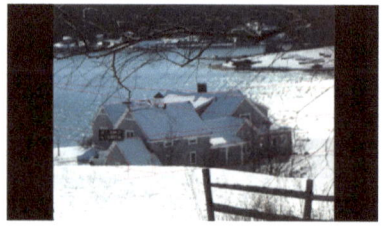

- **The Lighthouse Many Ways to Look At Things**
  https://vimeo.com/456594903

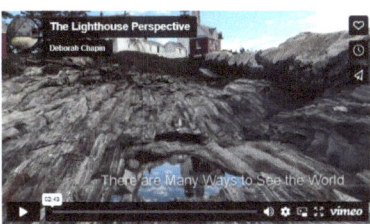

- **Drawing the Lighthouse at Perspective Study**
  https://vimeo.com/463088642

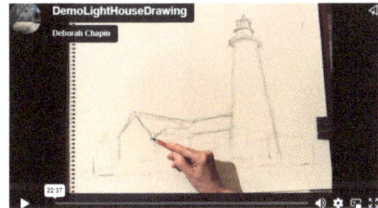

- **Short Simple Video Explanation of Dynamic Compositions**
  https://vimeo.com/454121803

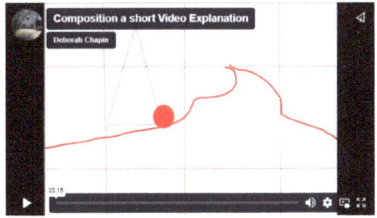

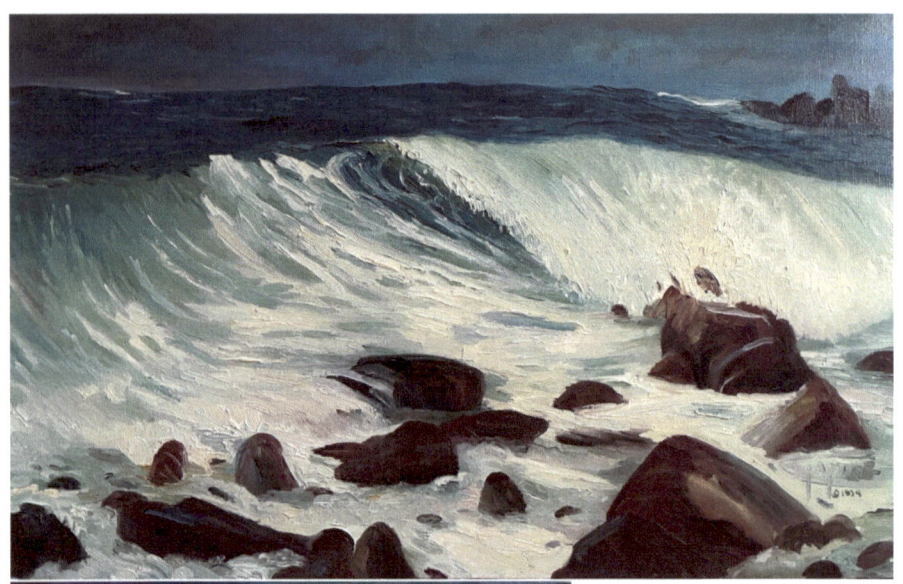

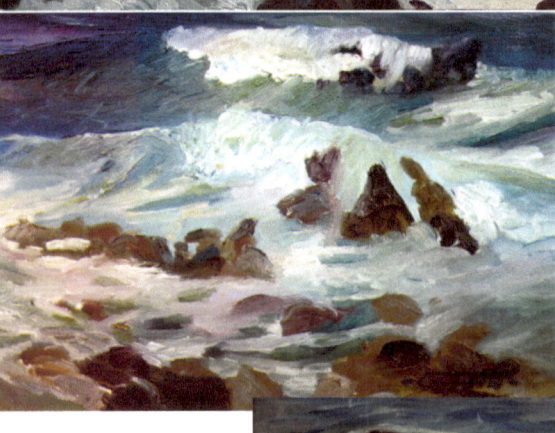

Research

Research for a painting begins in the mind of the artist. I have a log of ideas that I'd like to see realized in paint. To come up with this log an artist must first have some idea what can and cannot take place in nature. The latter is far less of worry then you might think and the former far more difficult to guess at without experience. Therefore, the more experience an artist has the more plausible the ideas become in the more successful an artist will find an idea realized in landscape, or Seascape etc.

When searching for a particular combination of elements such as Meander of the Sea, I knew that this particular combination of low tide in conjunction with dawn only occurs two times a month. I also knew that the underlined terrain of the harbor or in that must be shallow with beachy riverlets and not a steep drop off onto a depths of the sea. I also knew that if I wanted to accomplish a larger work, the location must be relatively easy to reach and not too far from where I slept. The sun rise at 5 AM and knowing that I am not likely to get up any earlier than 4:30 AM I wanted to be able to reach my location with a minimum of effort and time. It took three years to find the site, which had all these particular qualities and two years to find a house, which perfectly suited my location. In conclusion, there are plenty of reasons for not doing this type of painting. You will probably name several already, but ever so often you end up with a winner and there is nothing like the experience you will gain along the way.

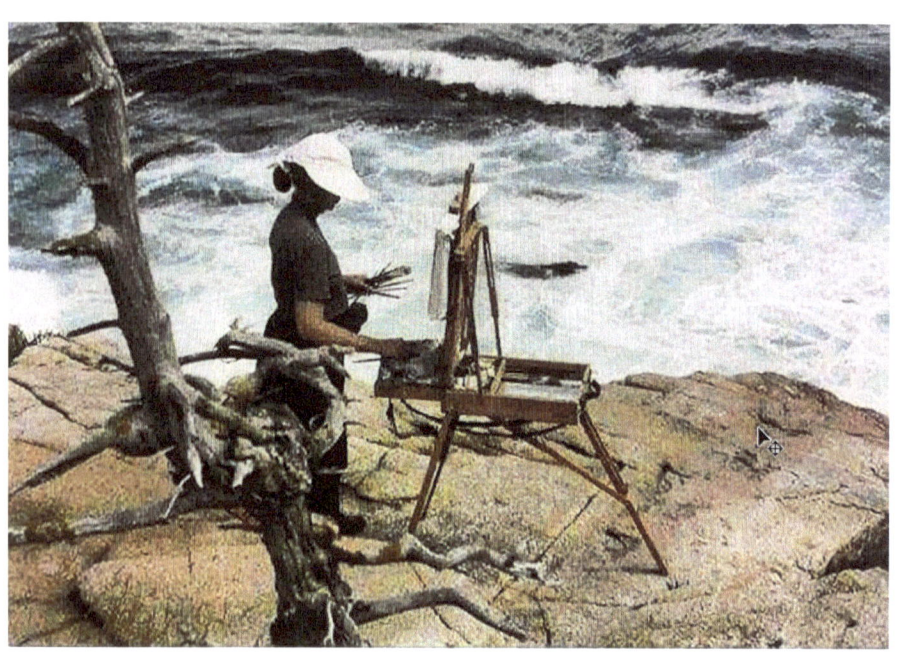

Advice to students

1. See every museum exhibition of the artist who painted during the last century that you can.

2. Be your own worst critic.

3. Never settle for what others thinks is good. Go beyond good.

4. Don't be happy with repeating yourself. Be adventurous.

5. Read everything relevant you can get your hands on. Be a critical reader and test what is written.

6. Sell your artwork but make improvements your artwork the goal, not satisfying the market. Sometimes you'll get lucky and can do both.

7. Buy the best materials you can afford, and present your work as professionally as you can.

8. Believe in your ability to become what you dream.

9. Listen to beautiful music for inspiration.

10. Pass on what you know. Sharing is contagious.

A discussion on form, value and color design inserted after the career thing

The following is a segment from Harold speeds discussion on value, form and color design, which I have found useful.

"What are the elements of visual image really? Form, tone and color. This is nothing new. We also could include design here as a separate element but I believe it might be more helpful to think in terms of form design, tone design and color design. Ah, so now you begin to decipher a world within a world…"

Instead of the student being first trained and drawing and afterwords acquiring a certain proficiency and painting I would suggest that each of the three divisions of the subject form tone and color be studied simultaneously from the start. They do not grow out of each other but rather into each other from three different centers. You will find as you advance in each of these three subjects that they will help each other. But in the form studies don't bother about the tone, concentrating on the form and likewise in the tone and color the important thing to learn is one thing well then practice it until you've mastered it. Heightened the effect that there is in all artistic work, and which is in a way I departure from Old accuracy, must not be made the excuse for careless and slovenly work. Intense honesty and the strictest accuracy always needed to catch the fleeting impression of the fine things seen by the artist…

Nature is not one to disclose her best to a shallow observer; she only reveals herself to those who seek hurry reverently, it is an inner sense and that arranges superficial visual appearances in tune with this indwelling spirit in nature.

This training of the observation and representation of what you see, is therefore the first thing you have to set up about, however Imaginative may be the kind of work you want to do. For if you cannot paint what you see, you will find yourself handicapped in trying to pay what you can imagine…

During the work the student has to be constantly king of the perceptions is calling up memory of the fine things seen. Nothing should be done when nothing fine is perceived. Never work without vision, without a perception of what you want to do ahead of what you have done. You will find that working for sometime on one part that the vision of what you wanted to do *was get style. Stop and go on with some other part, And where are you see what you want to do. Or if you do not see anything, stop and take up another canvas or rest. After change of work your I will see clearly what is wrong and what is wanted. Always turn your unfinished work to the wall since you see it with a fresh eye when you come to work on it again. when you go back to your location it to will show you fresh things if you have rested your eye... Keep in mind that the study of nature is the study of the instrument with which you are to express yourself. In the same way and finalist pay plays his scales, so as to acquire the capacity of producing pure tones on his instrument, training the year to appreciate Accurately the intervals between the different notes. So to the painter trains his eye or her eye to perceive accurately the appearances on his retina, and trains his hand to express accurately these perceptions. Play the scales is not music nor is it training the eye art but without this training we have no control of the means by which artistic things are done. If you gave a person a strong musical genius a violin to play, one who had never had any academic training for fear of spoiling his original genius, it is possible he might stumble upon some new and interesting music among a lot of noise that was executing. But this would be a very barbarous method of preserving originality. And the originality that is so delicate and order that is cannot stand the course of academic training, is so poor thing that is were better not considered"*

Oil Painting Techniques and Materials

by Harold Speed.

About this career

There are questions which students Considering this career frequently ask me. I know I would have appreciated some of these insights early on so here goes. They're not in any particular order.

1. **How do I limit what I see when working on site?** In making a selection of subject matter for your painting, decide first of all what particular objectives you want to accomplish. Are you preparing to practice an element of your work, or a completed piece or is something a scene appealing to you for some reason and if so what? Once you have decided that you can move on to the size of canvas and the speed at which you can execute it or if you are doing a larger work consider if it can be possible to finish, given the idea behind your work.

2. **How do I select a subject out of all the details that nature offers?** Once you have selected a subject, the size and have a clear idea why you're working, eliminate the items in the scene, which do not focus both you and the viewer on the objective of your work. It will occur to you as you are working and gaining experience, what elements you want to eliminate and what you want to keep in.

3. **Does advertising work?** Mass market advertising in general does not work. However, specifically targeted advertising to a particular group or area you are trying to reach does generally work with direct mail or google ads being the most sophisticated which are highly effective.   I would like to update this by saying that at this point in time that means to you or use and target specific markets if you know your demographics for the kind of buyer that buys your work.

4. **Do you do everything? Framing photography, preparing canvas?   How do you do it?** I section off my years into seasons. During the winter I take care of grunt work, preparing for the next season i.e. stretching canvas restocking supplies upgrading equipment photography the bulk of my work framing, advertising, website design and major changes, promotion and sales. During the

spring, summer and fall I concentrate on painting. Although some of the grunt work may need to be maintained during the painting season i.e. updating a newsletter or sending out materials which people request or portfolios to galleries, I focus on painting. During the winter when I'm working on grunt work I do some painting too but my focus is on getting the grunt work done. If we have the apprentice system still intact I would be happy because this would free up vast quantities of time.

5. **How do you do your photography?** I use to use tungsten 64T film with EBV bulbs. When I was photographing with medium format film, I would shoot 10 to 12 rolls at a time which would've been 24 per roll, so a lot of film. However, now that I have a digital camera I use my Canon EOS and I set up an easel, drape it with velvet and then set up light stands with umbrellas. At 45° angles to the painting, take a meter reading and voila! I could take only the photos that I want or need for a specific purpose and then make backup copies of the finished digital photo. I may also print it out in hi-res documentation or include it in a book such as this as a record. If you have a space that you can devote to your photography it would be ideal because much of your time is spent in setting up your equipment.

6. **You say you did your own website? What is involved?** Has it worked? That is the subject for another book or booklet at least. There's a lot to it and one had better be prepared to spend the time. Still I think it is a great tool and has a remarkable liberating effect. It is able to reach the market place directly; there are no barriers between you and the world and no one can cache your career simply because they are promoting a competitor. I believe it should be a tremendous benefit to the arts because of the competition. Those collectors who are trapped by the idea that only the establishment offers good works of art will be missing some of the best work out there. Yes it has worked marvelously. I use it to market my books, classes, introduce galleries and consultants and clients like my work. I can set up a portfolio posted up on the web to show specific works to private clients. I've sold paintings directly through it, a trend I expect to expand in the

coming years after the economy recuperates and previous collectors have used the website to introduce my work to their friends. I also am using it to preview or pre-sell shows. It is a great tool.

7. **Should I do a website myself or should I hire it done?** If you are a professional artist you should have a web presence. If you are an amateur, work on your art otherwise you may ruin your reputation before you get it started. So as a professional artist I believe that doing it yourself and developing and expanding it over time is the best route. But if you have no desire to do it and maintain it, hire it done. The disadvantage to this is that you cannot update your site on a whim nor can you follow many of the marketing suggestions I have mentioned in the above section because it can not be customized. Minimum price for a good website these days is $5000 up that quite a bit if you had hire it done. If you do it yourself, you'll need a computer, a scanner or digital camera, web connection, a URL or web address i.e. domain and some programs. I use A WordPress site for my website on my own server. It is not a free thing. I also use Filezilla for my FTP uploads and several apps on my WordPress site to facilitate the design of the pages. That is also a separate tutorial

8. **It seems that people travel a lot who paint on site? Is that a requirement?** If you live in a location that can afford you a lifetime of interesting subjects to paint then traveling can be kept to a minimum. That's why I moved to Maine. But if you don't happen to be lucky this way then yes you'll be traveling at least six months out of the year. Some years I made a trip to Maine, France, California then back up to Maine. The longer you can stay in one location the better. It can be very profitable because you can begin to know an area and that is when subtle subjects begin to reveal themselves and your best work will result. Best of all 2 to 3 month stay if you can stand it over a period of years. This is how I painted in France and I found it revealed more each year. Dealing with isolation can be a problem.

9. **What do you need in order to do your own framing?** You need a supplier of good molding, if you get stick molding which is the least expensive you'll need to have

a saw, I recommend Dewalt rotary saw with two braces on it too, and good leveling device and you'll need a good work bench on which to mount the saw plus a host of paraphernalia which will occur to you when you start setting up.

Suggested reading list read them all to complete the course

- The Artistic Anatomy of Trees by Rex Vicat Cole
- Landscape Painting by John Carlson
- Composition of Outdoor Painting by Edgar Payne
- The Painter Joaquin Sorolla by Edmund peel
- Bridgeman's life drawing by George Bridgman
- Oil Painting Techniques and Materials by Herald speed
- The New Painting Impressionism Exhibition Catalog by Fine Arts Museum of San Francisco and National Gallery Art Washington DC
- Perspective for Artists by Rex Vicat Cole
◦ The Photographic Image by Virgil Elliot
◦ A Studio of Her Own by Erica Hirshler S
◦ Mary Cassatt a life by Nancy Mowell
◦ Overcoming All Obstacles the Women of Academy Julian by Jane R. Becker
◦ Art, Perception, and Reality by E. H. Gombrich, Julian Hochberg, and Max black
◦ Visual thinking by Rudolph Arnheim
◦ American Arts Quarterly published by Newton-Cropsey Foundation

About the Artist

Select Exhibition History of Deborah Chapin Museum Exhibitions, include Ketter Kunst Germany, Grand Palais Paris, CM Russell Museum, Talks at the Smithsonian National Museum of American Art among others:

- **Grand Prize Winner,** Paint America touring exhibition, St. George Art Museum, St. George, UT July- September 2007, 2008.
- **CM Russell Art Auction,** CM Russell Museum, Great Falls, MT — March 2007 **NAPA Valley Museum, Arts for the Parks 2004,** Yountville, California — June-September 2005 **Kolb Studio, Grand Canyon Association,** Arts for the Parks 2004, Grand Canyon, Arizona — April-June 2005 Booth Western Art **Museum, Arts for the Parks 2004,** Cartersville, Georgia — December 2004- February 2005
- **Ketterer Kunst Hamburg,** 17th- 20th Century Marine art — 252. Auction, — Sept 2000. (see KettererPresscatalogue.htm and KetterKunstCatalogue.html
- **Louvre** — Salon de Société Nationale des Beaux Arts, Paris — June 1999, 2000, 2001
- **Meridian International Center,** One-Person Exhibition -1997, 1992.
- **Grand Palais ,** Paris, France — 1993, 1994, 2003.
- **Colorado Historical Museum,** "Artists of America Exhibition", Denver, CO — 1988, 1990. (catalogues published)
- **Maryland Historical Museum,** Baltimore, MD — 1989.
- **San Diego Maritime Museum,** One-Person Exhibit — 1988.
- **Carnegie Art Museum,** One-Person Exhibit — 1988.Ventura County Maritime Museum, One-Person Exhibit. 1988.Mariners Museum, Fremantle, Western Australia — 1986.

Publications:

- biographical sketch is featured in the: **Allgemeines Kunstlerlexikon** (dictionary of artists), published by Saur in Leipzig, GE v. 15; fall 1997 which is the standard for reference of museum's worldwide. It is a complete and exact biographical data spanning the entire world-wide spectrum of arts from antiquity up to present with over 300,000 artists and a selection of exhibitions by these artists based on the structured data of the encyclopedia Thieme-Becker and Vollmer (the predecessors of the AKL) complete from a to z and the structured data of the AKL as the printed version goes on. currently from a to "campagnari". data from Allgemeines Künstlerlexikon, published in printed form by K. G. Saur Verlag.
- **Smithsonian American Art Museum,** Invited to Lecture/DVD Demo on Plein Air Painting, Sea & Surf en Plein Air, Washington, DC, October 2007.
- **CM Russell Musem,** Charles M Russell Museum catalog Exhibition/ Auction, Montana, p 19, 63, 2007.
- **Chesapeake Life,** January 2007, Shorelines Feature p29. Review of — "On Location" by R. Mcdaniel, 2005.
- **Gerlinde de Beer (auth), monograph, Ludolf Backhuysen,** p.56, 2001.
- **Who's Who in American Art,** 24th — 31st edition 2001-2016. Lifetime Achievement Award 2021.
- **Ketterer Kunst Hamburg Maritime Kunst Catalogue,** Hamburg, GE - Auction 2 Sept, 2000.
- **International Artist, Masters Painters of the World,** "Etude des Roches", Australia — J
- **Allgemeines Kunstlerlexikon** (dictionary of artists), published by Saur in Leipzig, GE v. 15; fall 1997.
- **American Artist Magazine,** Sea & Surf en Plein Air, NYC — October 1995 (copies available).
- **Artists of America,** catalogue, Colorado Historical Museum, 1988,1990.
- **Exposition Catalogue,** Catalogue Listing. Salon des Ind`ependants, Paris — 1993,1994.
- **US Art,** interview by Gillian Judge, Adams publishing, Minnesota, December 1990.
- **Chesapeake Bay Magazine,** Chesapeake communications, Maryland, May 1983, May 1990.

- **Dictionary of Sea Painters**, book by Edward Archibald, London – June 1989.
- American Artist magazine, Billboard Publications, NYC – January 1988.
- **Yacht Portraits,** book published by Sheridan press/overseas press, Milan, IT – October 1987.

Galleries:

- **Women Painting Women** – RJD Gallery, Sag Harbor, NY – October 2015
- **Mystic International** – Mystic Seaport – Mystic, Connecticut – September 2007, 1985, 1984, 1983
- **Paint America** – Indian Summer, Winner of the inaugural Paint America Competition – 2007,
- **The Natural World Observed** – N.A.P.P.A.P. National Exhibition – Texas Art Gallery – Dallas, Texas – February 2007
- **Southeastern Wildlife Exposition,** Charleston, SC February 2005-2008.
- **The Natural World Observed** – N.A.P.P.A.P. National Exhibition – Elkhorn Gallery – Winterpark, Colorado – June 2006
- **Ella Carothers Dunnegan Gallery** – Bolivar, Missouri – March 2005
- **The Natural World Observed** – N.A.P.P.A.P. National Exhibition – National Arts Club – New York – September 2005
- **Arts for the Parks Top 100 and Finalist,** Art West Gallery and Jackson Lake Lodge Jackson Lake Lodge, Jackson Hole, Wyoming – September – December 2001, 2004.
- **National Arts Club** – Gregg Gallery, One-Person Exhibition, New York – September 1998, 2003, 2005
- **Audubon Naturalist Society**, One-Person Exhibitions – 1992, 1994, 1995, 2002.
- **Northwest Marine Art Exhibition,** Kirsten Gallery – 2002, 2004, 2006.
- **Impressions of New England** – Bennington VT – 2002, 2003.
- **Beaux Arts Bash**, Scottsdale Artist School, Scottsdale, AZ – 2001-2008.
- **Southern Vermont Art Center,** One Person Exhibition – June, 2000.
- **Annual Exhibiting Artist Members'** Exhibition, National Arts Club, 1998-2006.
- **Salmagundi Open,** Salmagundi Club, NYC – 1996. Grand National, American Artists Professional League, Salmagundi Club, NYC – 1995.

- Baku, Azerbaijan (formerly in USSR), American Embassy-1995-98.
- Bogota, Colombia, American Embassy -1995-98. (Catalog Published)
- Sanaa, Yemen, American Embassy – 1995-98.
- Quito, Ecuador, American Embassy – 1993-96. United Arab Emirates,
- Abu Dhabi, American Embassy – 1992-95. (Catalog Published)

- National Arts Club
- National Academy of Professional Plein Air Painters (founder)
- Artist Fellowship Artist
- Societe Nationale des Beaux Arts

Career Quotes

"One thing you have that makes us old-timers sit up and take notice is your <u>nerve</u>. You attempt the impossible and it comes off so completely that in your "paintings" the impossible looks easy... It is this courage, nerve, and your ability to execute your bold concepts which puts your work in the fore-front among all other young painters"

Fred Freeman
December 1983

*"You work is so amazing,
you really understand sailing and water."*

Jack Sutphen
*Support Staff "Star's & Stripes"
Fremantle, Western Australia 1988*

The Maryland Historical Society is pleased to have the opportunity to show your fine work at the American Society of Marine Artists Exhibit...the exhibit with almost 900 guests present was the most successful such event we have ever held...

Jennifer T. Goldsborough
*Chief Curator
April 1989*

"You paint water better than anyone I've ever seen"

Peter Orvis
*Naval Consultant
1988*

"I am so pleased I was able to collect your work"

Charles E Pardoe
*Pardoe Properties
1992*

"Your work is the only representative of the 20th century in this marine art exhibition."

Gelinde de Beer
Historian, Author and
Curator for Ketter Kunst Exhibition
2000

"It is a fine and valuable book! Your words are helpful, instructive and practical. Certainly a must for artists approaching painting out of doors. I'm grateful to have a copy!

Raymond Kinstler
2000

"I don't think you ever received the recognition you deserved."

Syd Porter
President of Porter Consultants, Inc., a health physics consulting firm
2004

"Thank you for all you have done Debbie. It is much appreciated."

Gary Jobson
America's Cup Tactician and ESPN
St Michaels 2005

"I am so honored to have a copy of your beautiful book on plein air painting Debbie, great work! Thank you so much."

Virginia Mecklenburg Sr Curator
Smithsonian American Art Museum
2009

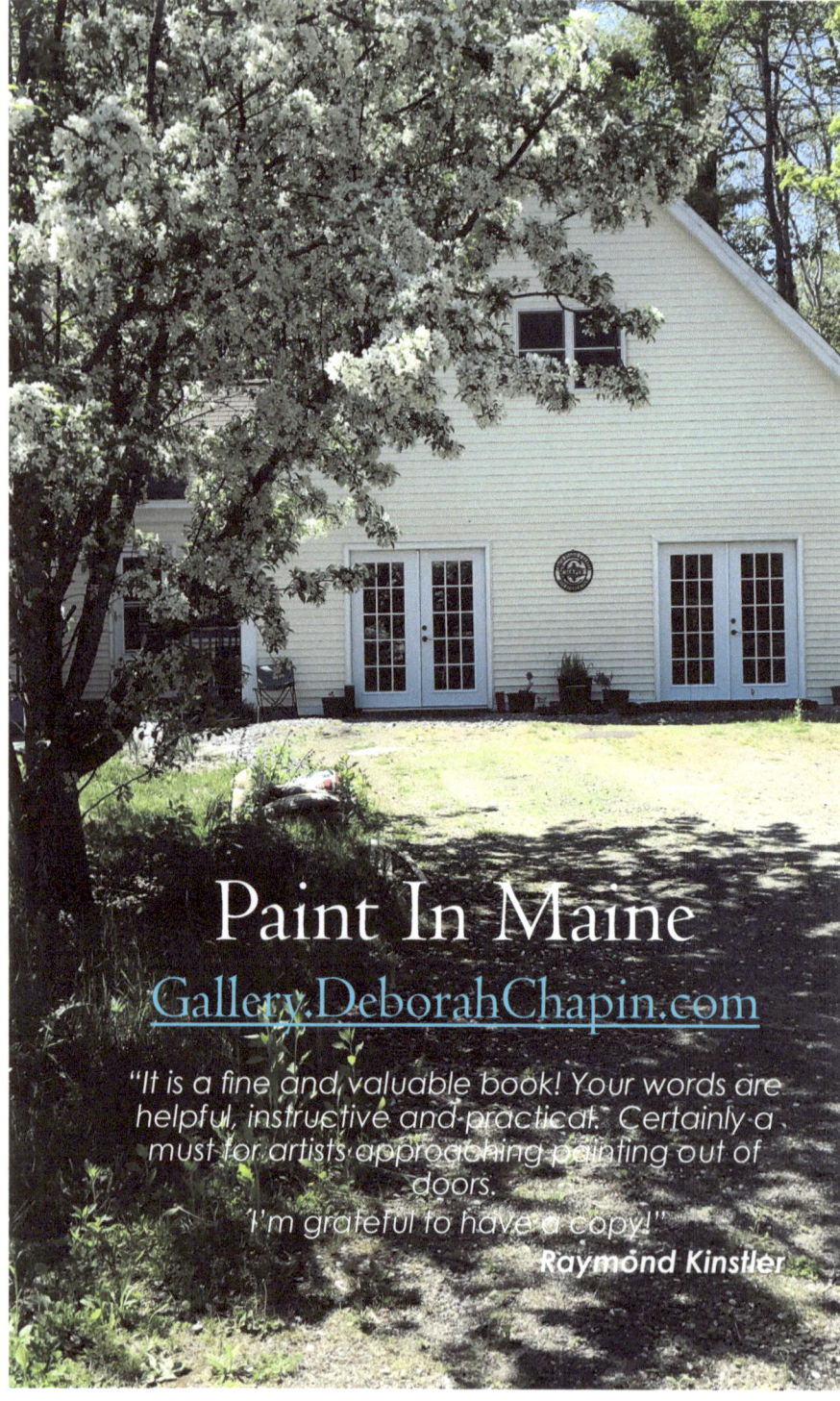

Paint In Maine

Gallery.DeborahChapin.com

"It is a fine and valuable book! Your words are helpful, instructive and practical. Certainly a must for artists approaching painting out of doors.
I'm grateful to have a copy!"
Raymond Kinstler

www.ingramcontent.com/pod-product-compliance
Lightning Source LLC
Chambersburg PA
CBHW040905180526
45159CB00010BA/2938